Lovable Soft Toys

Jennifer MacLennan

D1307046

 Sterling Publishing Co., Inc.   New York

Library of Congress Cataloging-in-Publication Data

MacLennan, Jennifer.
  Lovable soft toys.

  Includes index.
  1. Soft toy making. I. Title.
TT174.3.M33 1985 745.592′4 85−10080
ISBN 0−8069−5726−3
ISBN 0−8069−6240−2 (pbk.)

Copyright © 1985 by Jennifer MacLennan
Published by Sterling Publishing Co., Inc.
Two Park Avenue, New York, N.Y. 10016
Distributed in Australia by Capricorn Book Co. Pty. Ltd.
Unit 5C1 Lincoln St., Lane Cove, N.S.W. 2066
Distributed in the United Kingdom by Blandford Press
Link House, West Street, Poole, Dorset BH15 ILL, England
Distributed in Canada by Oak Tree Press Ltd.
% Canadian Manda Group, P.O. Box 920, Station U
Toronto, Ontario, Canada M8Z 5P9

Contents

ACKNOWLEDGMENTS 4

1 Materials and Techniques 5

2 Simple Circle Designs 13

3 Toys Made from Simple Shapes 22

4 Bears and Rabbits 39

5 Dolls 64

6 Beard Dolls 88

7 Christmas Toys 109

8 Lions and Tigers 121

METRIC CHART 126

INDEX 127

ABOUT THE AUTHOR 128

Color illustrations opposite page 32

Acknowledgments

The thanks owed for this volume are both direct and indirect, for help, inspiration, and support I've received over many years and from some very special people. First, thanks to three very special kids—Sheena, Gwen, and Shaun. Thanks to my parents, for all their interest and encouragement: to Dad, for stuffing whales, and Mum, for not telling me about the monster arms! Thanks also to Doh, for inspiration and the Hourglass; to Brock, for moral support; to Isobel, for her encouragement in the writing of this book; to Moo, for all her faith in me, many years ago; and to Tim, for believing in this when I didn't, and for the help with the photography. And to Ellen, wherever she is, thanks from the Puppet Lady.

I would also like to express my gratitude to Dennis, for the helpful advice he so willingly and generously provided me.

Finally, this book is for Jimbo, without whose patience, support, and unflagging enthusiasm the toys in it would never have been created. Here's to you, Monse.

—Jen

1 Materials and Techniques

Soft-toy making is one of the most rewarding hobbies of all. It is, in comparison to other hobbies, reasonable in cost and can be undertaken with equipment found in most homes. It can be as simple or as complex a challenge as desired, according to the ability of the craftsperson. Probably the best part, however, is that it produces a tangible, useful result: There is satisfaction in creating a well-made, appealing, personal item that will give pleasure to someone who will, in all likelihood, cherish the toy for many years.

My aim is to introduce the beginner to the craft of toy making, and also to present a measure of challenge to those who already have some experience in the craft. The toys in this book range from very simple to more advanced, and there should be something here for everyone.

Basic Equipment

For making soft toys, most of the equipment which you might have from other home sewing projects will do, with a few additions. If you've never done any sewing and don't have all the equipment, don't despair. Substitutions can often be made. Here is a list of equipment needed to make soft toys:

- Scissors: a pair for paper and a good sharp pair for fabric. Thread snips are helpful too, but not essential.
- Dressmaker's chalk and a permanent marker.
- Pen and pencil.
- Needles for hand sewing: The closing up of toys and attaching of extraneous parts is done by hand. A curved

upholstery needle may be useful for attaching noses, eyes, etc.

- Strong thread for closing toys and attaching appendages.
- Pins: the glass-headed kind are best.
- Fabric adhesive: Any fabric adhesive will do.
- A sewing machine: Most of the toys in this book are machine constructed as far as possible for strength and durability. It is possible to sew all by hand, however, provided you are careful and work with strong, firm backstitching.
- Cardboard: Bristol board or cereal-box cardboard will do for patterns. This is easier to work with than paper, especially if you intend to reuse your patterns.
- A length of dowel, or an unsharpened pencil, for stuffing.
- A drawing compass, for making circular patterns.

Previous experience with sewing is helpful but not essential, since the techniques used in making toys are somewhat different from those used for dressmaking. With care and patience, however, anyone should be able to reproduce the designs in this book by following the directions carefully.

Materials

Fabrics

The principal fabrics that I use for toys are fake fur and felt. Fur is available in a wide variety of bright colors, and is washable and soft-textured. The longer piled fur is useful for wigs and hair, and I use it extensively for that purpose, since I like its effect better than that of yarn. Both are available at any fabric or crafts shop.

Felt is versatile, colorful, and non-woven, so it does not fray. I use it mainly for features or small articles of clothing, but not usually for an entire toy, since it is not really washable except with extreme care. It has a tendency to fade and stretch out of shape if not handled with caution.

It would hold up fine as a well-secured feature on a toy of another fabric (such as paw pads on a furry animal), but is not, in my opinion, best for the construction of entire toys, especially if they are to be played with by energetic kids.

For some of the toys discussed, such as dolls, cotton broadcloths or blends are recommended. In all cases, you may want to substitute fabric similar in weight and thickness. This is just one of the ways in which you can make the toys expressions of your own creative energy, and is to be encouraged wherever possible.

Eyes

Several of the toys are made with purchased plastic lock-in eyes. These come in a variety of styles, sizes, and colors, and may be purchased from crafts suppliers and notions departments. They are child-safe when properly applied, and give toys a professional look. They are ap-

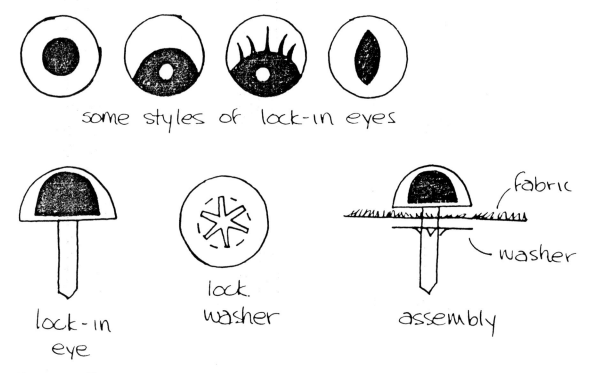

some styles of lock-in eyes

lock-in eye

lock. washer

fabric

washer

assembly

Fig. 1.   *Different types of lock-in eyes and assembly techniques.*

plied as follows: Patterns using these eyes will have dots marked on the face to indicate eye placement. When the face has been assembled, snip holes for eye stems where marked, making sure eyes are even. Push stems through holes from the right side, and secure with safety washers.

Other eye styles used here include paste-on plastic moving eyes, available in sizes from 4 mm to 28 mm. These are attached to the toy with glue. If you cannot find these eyes for one reason or another, you may want to substitute felt eyes for your toy. Several of the toys here have felt eyes and may serve as inspiration for your creations.

Stuffing

There are various types of stuffing available, but in some countries you are going to be restricted pretty much to either foam chips or polyester fibre, which can be found in fabric or crafts shops. The latter is by far the most suitable: It is clean, easy to use, non-allergenic, washable, and gives a nice firm finish. Foam chips, although adequate for large furry toys, give a lumpy finish to toys such as dolls, with a thin cotton skin. They are also messy to work with and difficult to pack firmly. You can use shredded (clean) old pantyhose, but it's difficult to save enough to fill large toys and it is awfully heavy. Also, government regulations require that toys for sale be filled with new materials, so if you're making your toys for commercial purposes you cannot use this kind of stuffing.

Techniques

General Directions

These general directions will apply to all of the toys discussed, and are useful guides for you to use when working on your own designs and variations. Read this section very carefully before proceeding with toys in the following chapters.

PATTERNS: In most cases, full-size patterns are provided for the toys and should be traced and mounted on cardboard. You will find this step worthwhile, since the cardboard patterns are easier to trace around than paper ones.

LAYOUTS: Fabric amounts quoted are usually the minimum amounts for each toy and are based on the most economical layouts. No layouts will be given, but it's not hard to work out your own using the following method. Cut toy patterns from a single layer of fabric, to avoid distortion (for this reason also, pattern pieces are never pinned to fabric). Trace around the pattern pieces with marker or chalk onto the wrong side of the fabric; begin with the larger pieces and fit the smaller ones in around them. On fur fabric, place each piece so that the nap runs in the direction of the arrows on the pattern pieces. (To determine the nap direction, stroke the fabric. If it feels smooth, you are stroking with the nap.) Remember to reverse the pattern for pieces that are sewn in pairs (arms, legs, and body front and back). On felt you need not worry about grain, so no arrows are provided on pieces meant to be cut from felt. In this instance, use the most economical layout, laying pieces in any direction. Arrows given on other pattern pieces (those meant for ordinary unnapped woven fabric) are grain lines; they are used in the same fashion as those on commercial patterns. (In other words, the arrows run parallel to the selvedges.)

CUTTING OUT: Cut all pieces out carefully along traced lines. On fur pieces, try to avoid cutting through the pile on the front by snipping through the backing only with the point of the scissors.

STITCHING: When stitching toys, *always* baste using a running stitch first, and fit the pieces together carefully. Fur fabric has a tendency to stretch and distort during stitching, so this preliminary basting *should not be skipped!* Handle fabric carefully—a careful fitting together of pieces is the only way to be sure that a properly shaped toy results from your efforts, and it's far better to spend a little extra time in the preliminary stages than to rip out stitching to do over. Stitch with a fine stitch, with a large needle (Nos. 16−18) in your machine, or by hand with strong firm backstitching.

For those unfamiliar with the terms running stitch and backstitch, let me clarify them. A running stitch is basically a small, even stitch usually run on a needle in groups. A backstitch is basically a hand stitch made by inserting the needle a stitch length to the right and bringing it up an equal distance to the left.

NOTE: A ¼″ seam allowance is provided on all toys unless otherwise indicated.

Fig. 2. Cross-section and top view of a backstitch.

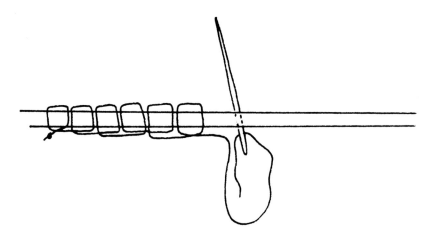

backstitch

cross-section: two fabric layers

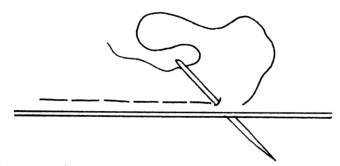

top view: close to edge of fabric

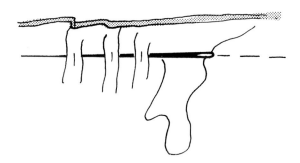

Fig. 3. Running stitch.

TURNING: Clip all corners and trim curves. Turn toy through opening, being sure to turn small parts such as fingers, noses, snouts, toes, etc., first. For this job you will find the length of dowel or an unsharpened pencil useful.

STUFFING: When you're stuffing a toy, fill the extremities such as fingers, toes, cheeks, shoulders, etc., first. Use small pieces of stuffing and push down with a length of dowel or a pencil. Fill the toy carefully and firmly—don't skimp! You'll be surprised how much stuffing it will take, because it packs pretty firmly, but persevere, because a properly stuffed toy not only looks much better, it lasts a lot longer.

CLOSING UP: Although I've tried to work as far as possible by machine, you will at some time have to hand sew your toys—to close them or to attach limbs, etc. The stitch I use for this is the ladder stitch. It's similar to a running stitch, with alternating stitches taken in either side of the fabric, as shown in Fig. 4. When you pull up on your thread the stitches disappear into the fabric; therefore, no threads are visible or accessible to small, inquisitive fingers.

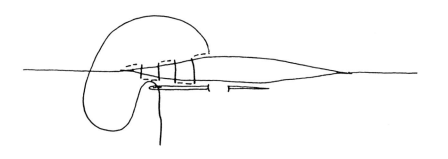

Fig. 4. Ladder stitch.

GROOMING: Most fur toys may be groomed after finishing by picking out with a pin any fur which may be trapped in the seams. Give the toy a good brushing.

It should be emphasized again that before moving on to make any of the toys in the following chapters, you should read over these general directions carefully and follow each step for your chosen toy. This will help ensure that your efforts are rewarded with success. Now, on to your first creations!

Enlarging and Transferring Patterns

Patterns for a few of the toys are too large to reproduce in this book. Therefore, they have been reduced by either 25% or 50% and printed on top of a ¾ inch or ½ inch grid. To enlarge these patterns so you can use the sizes of materials given in the directions, buy 1 inch grid paper or make your own. Copy the pattern square by square from the grid in the book onto the large grid paper. After enlarging the pattern in this way, cut it out and continue instructions for making the pattern.

2 Simple Circle Designs

The simplest of all toy designs begins with a circle of fabric, gathered up into a ball and stuffed. Once completed, the balls can be joined in combinations to produce the simple but effective toys in this chapter. From then on circle designing will be used in later chapters to form parts of larger toys—noses, tails, eyes, etc.

The toys in this chapter are made from circles of fur fabric and felt in diameters of 1, 3, 4 and 5 inches (2.5, 7.5, 10 and 12.5 cm), with features made of tiny felt dots. It is best at the beginning not to attempt circle toys much larger than these, since it's hard to make them smooth and without ridges. Also, for many the effect would be lost with larger dimensions. These small toys will give the beginner an opportunity to practise toy making and use up small scraps of fabric. The largest of these take only two small circles, and all can be made from small remnants of fabric.

Basic Circle Technique

• Cut out the circle from your chosen fabric. • With a double length of thread in a hand needle, run a gathering thread all around the outside edge of the circle. • Pull up gently on the thread with right side of fabric to outside until the circle begins to curl up into a ball. • Stuff as you go with plenty of filling, making sure the ball is firm and without ridges. • Pull the thread tight and secure with a few stitches.

Once you've made the basic ball shape, you can then join it with a ladder stitch to other balls to make the toys that follow.

For most of these toys, you will be making a round ball shape; for others you will want your ball slightly oval. This is achieved by moulding the ball with your hand as you stuff.

Fig. 5. Run a gathering stitch around the outside edge of the circle.

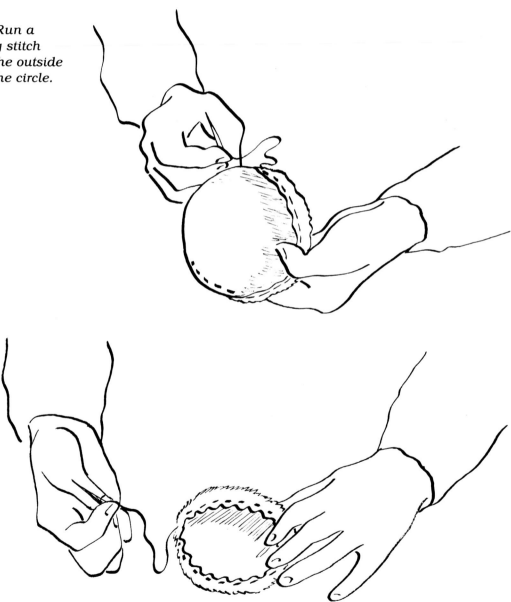

Fig. 6. Pull up on thread so edges begin to curl to inside (wrong side).

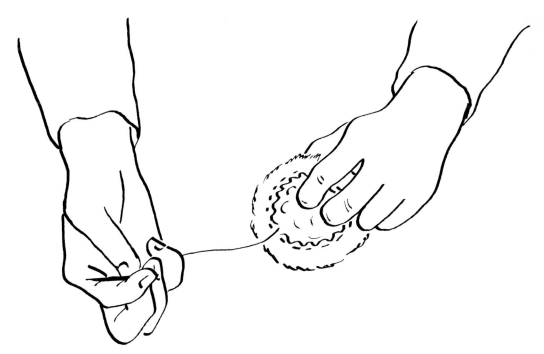

Fig. 7.   As you pull up on thread, push stuffing into center of ball, filling completely.

Fig. 8.   Pull thread up tightly to close ball and knot.

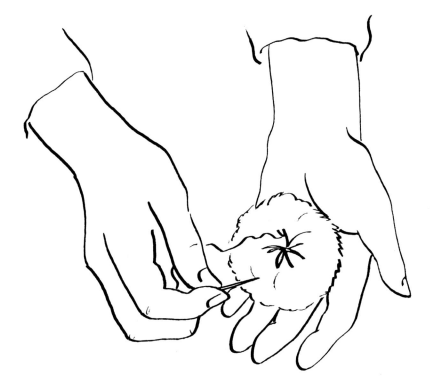

Toys Made From One Ball

Mouse

Fig. 9.   Mouse, Frog and Lady Bug.

Material: *3" circle of white fur*
¼ x 4" strip of white fur for tail
base of pink felt
ears of white felt
scraps of pink and black felt for ear linings,
     eyes, nose
small amount of stuffing

Make oval-shaped ball of white fur. Glue tail under body and glue base to bottom, enclosing tail so it protrudes from back end of mouse. Stitch base to bottom of mouse. Glue pink ear linings to white ears. Glue ears to front body. Glue small black dots for eyes and tiny triangle for nose.

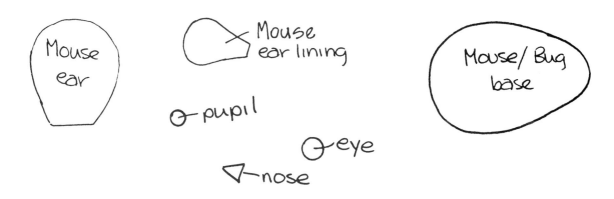

Fig. 10.   Patterns for Mouse.

Frog

Material: *4" circle of green fur*
flippers of green felt
two 1" circles of white felt
1" circle of green felt
scraps of yellow, red, and black felt
small amount of stuffing

Make ball of green fur. Glue and sew to flippers. Split green-felt circle. Glue one half of green circle over each white circle to form eyelid. Make eyeball by basic circle technique. Add tiny black pupils to eyeballs. Glue and stitch eyeballs to head. Glue smiling red mouth cut from a strip of red felt to front of frog, and yellow dots to back.

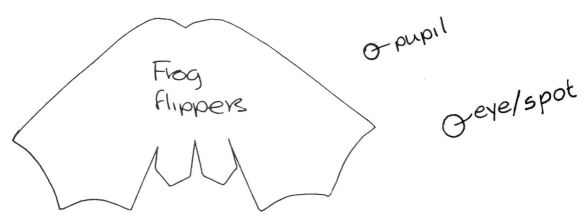

Fig. 11.   Patterns for Frog.

Lady Bug

Material: *3″ circle of red fur*
scraps of black felt for base, face, dots,
   pupils
scraps of white felt for eyes
small amount of stuffing

Make oval-shaped ball of red fur. Glue bottom to base and hand stitch all around. Glue face piece over one end of bug. Glue 4 dots to bug back. Make eyes of white felt and black dots and glue to face.

Fig. 12.   Patterns for Lady Bug.

Spider

Fig. 13.   Spider and Bee.

Material: *5″ circle of fur (any color)*
3″ circle of felt (to coordinate)
scraps of red, white, and black felt for
tongue and eyes
3 long chenille stems
small amount of stuffing
optional: length elastic thread and one
elastic band

Make flattened ball of colored fur. Tie bundle of stems together in middle. Spread to form 6 legs. Glue ball to legs and base over legs to bottom of ball so that legs protrude. Hand stitch base to body. Bend stems into leg shapes. Glue tongue and eyes to front face.

Spider may be made to hang if desired by running elastic thread up middle and attaching elastic band.

Fig. 14. Patterns for Spider.

Toys Made From Two Balls

For the basic body shape required for these toys, make two balls, one slightly smaller than the other, as described in the basic technique section (pages 13 to 15). Put dab of glue on raw edges, and join two balls together with ladder stitch, enclosing raw seams between.

Bee

Material: *3″ circle of black fur*
4″ circle of gold fur
1″ circle of black felt
small amount of black felt, cut in ¼″ strips
for stripes

1" circle of gold felt
scrap of pink felt
1 pair of paste-on moving eyes, 10 mm
wings of white felt (cut 4)

Make basic body from black and gold fur. Glue black 1" circle to bottom of bee, and glue two stripes in place around body. Make nose by circle method and stitch to face. Glue eyes in place. Glue pink heart to left breast. Glue wings together in pairs. Topstitch edge by hand or machine. Attach to bee in back.

Fig. 15.   Patterns for Bee. See photo on page 18.

Snowman

Fig. 16. Snowman dressed for the cold weather.

Material: *3" and 4" circles of white fur*
scraps of orange and black felt for nose, eyes,
buttons, mouth
scrap of striped fabric for scarf
small amount of stuffing
small plastic top hat

Make basic body of white fur. Cut carrot nose of orange felt. Fold so straight edges meet, and stitch, leaving curved top open. Turn and stuff. Gather top opening and pull closed. Stitch to face. Glue dots for eyes, mouth, buttons. Tie striped fabric around neck for scarf. Glue top hat to head.

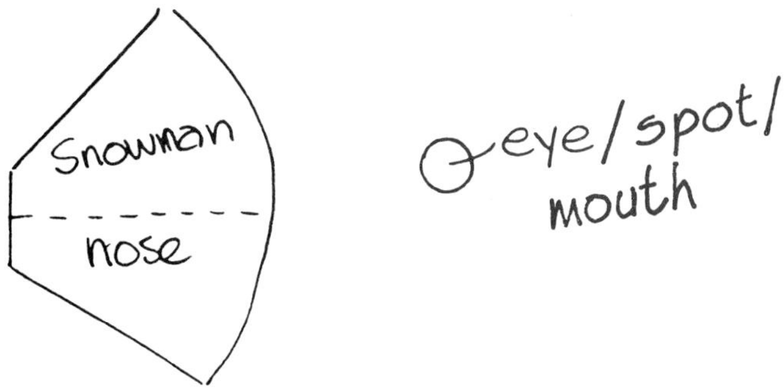

Snowman
nose

eye/spot/
mouth

Fig. 17.   Patterns for Snowman.

3 Toys Made From Simple Shapes

The next logical step from circle designing moves us into a group of toys made from various simple shapes. Some of these have been adapted into a variety of animals with a few adjustments in features. Those shown are just a few of the possibilities, and by combining these shapes with the techniques of Chapter 2, endless variations can be achieved.

Before proceeding, reread Chapter 1.

Goony Bird

Fig. 18. Even though you can't see its mouth, this Goony Bird is all smiles.

Material: 3 x 5" long-pile fur for body
5" square of contrasting felt for beak, feet
1 pair paste-on moving eyes, 15 mm
small amount of stuffing

Right sides facing, stitch darts in body pieces. Place 2
sides together, right sides facing, and stitch all around
curved edge, leaving bottom edge open. Turn right-side
out and stuff. Brush hair out of way and gather bottom
closed. Flatten bottom and glue body to feet with seam
down center front. Comb hair into pleasing shape and
glue beak to front. Glue eyes in position.

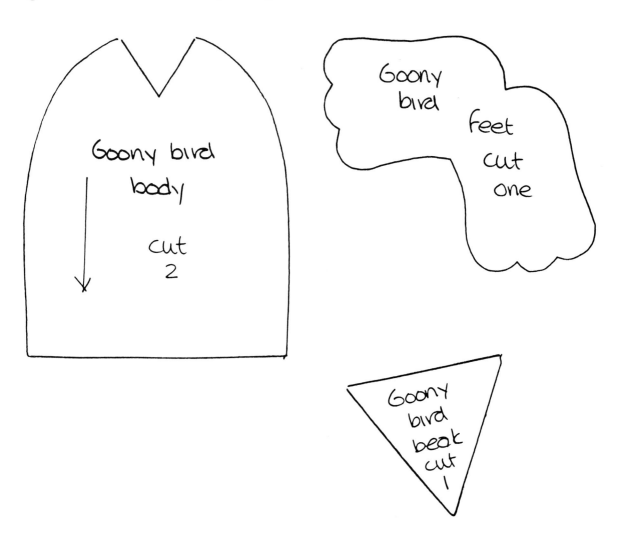

Fig. 19.   Feet, beak, and body patterns for Goony Bird.

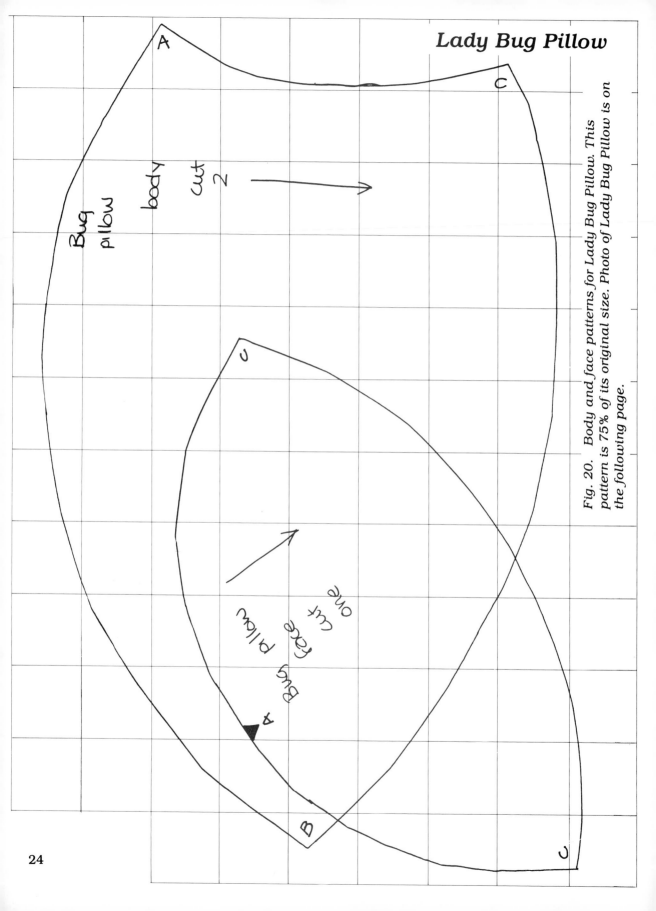

Fig. 20. Body and face patterns for Lady Bug Pillow. This pattern is 75% of its original size. Photo of Lady Bug Pillow is on the following page.

Lady Bug Pillow

Bug
pillow

body

cut
2

Bug pillow
face
cut
one

A

B

C

A

C

C

Fig. 21.   This Lady Bug Pillow has a quizzical expression.

Material: *14" square of red fur for body*
8 x 12" black fur for face
5 x 6" black felt for dots, pupils
2 x 4" white felt for eyes
13" square black broadcloth for base
8 oz. stuffing

Right sides facing, stitch body back A-B. Matching notch A to seam line, right sides facing, stitch face to body C-A-C. Stitch bug back to base, right sides facing, leaving about 3 inches open at back. Turn right-side out and stuff. Close opening by hand. Glue 4 black dots to back and eyes to front of face. If desired, eyes and dots may be hand stitched in place.

Fig. 22.   Eye and pupil patterns for Lady Bug Pillow.

Chicken with Variations

Fig. 23.   Chicken (far right) is greeted by a carrot-clutching Rabbit and a Bluebird. Instructions for making the Rabbit and Bluebird can be found on pages 28, 29, and 30.

Fig. 24.   Eye and beak patterns for Chicken.

CHICKEN:

Material: 8 x 9" yellow fur for body
4 x 6" orange felt for feet/beak
scrap of black felt for eyes
1 matching fluff feather
1 oz. stuffing

Stitch wings together in pairs, right sides facing, leaving tops open. Turn but do not stuff. Matching edges, baste in place indicated on body front. Sew body darts. Baste feather in place at top of head.

Right sides facing, stitch body front to body back, leaving open at bottom and catching wings and feather in line of stitching. Turn and stuff. Close bottom by hand.

Topstitch feet together in pairs, wrong sides facing, leaving open at heel. Stuff lightly without turning, and sew closed. Attach to bottom of body.

Make top and bottom beak by topstitching together in pairs, wrong sides facing. Glue and sew to face. Stick eye dots to face just above beak.

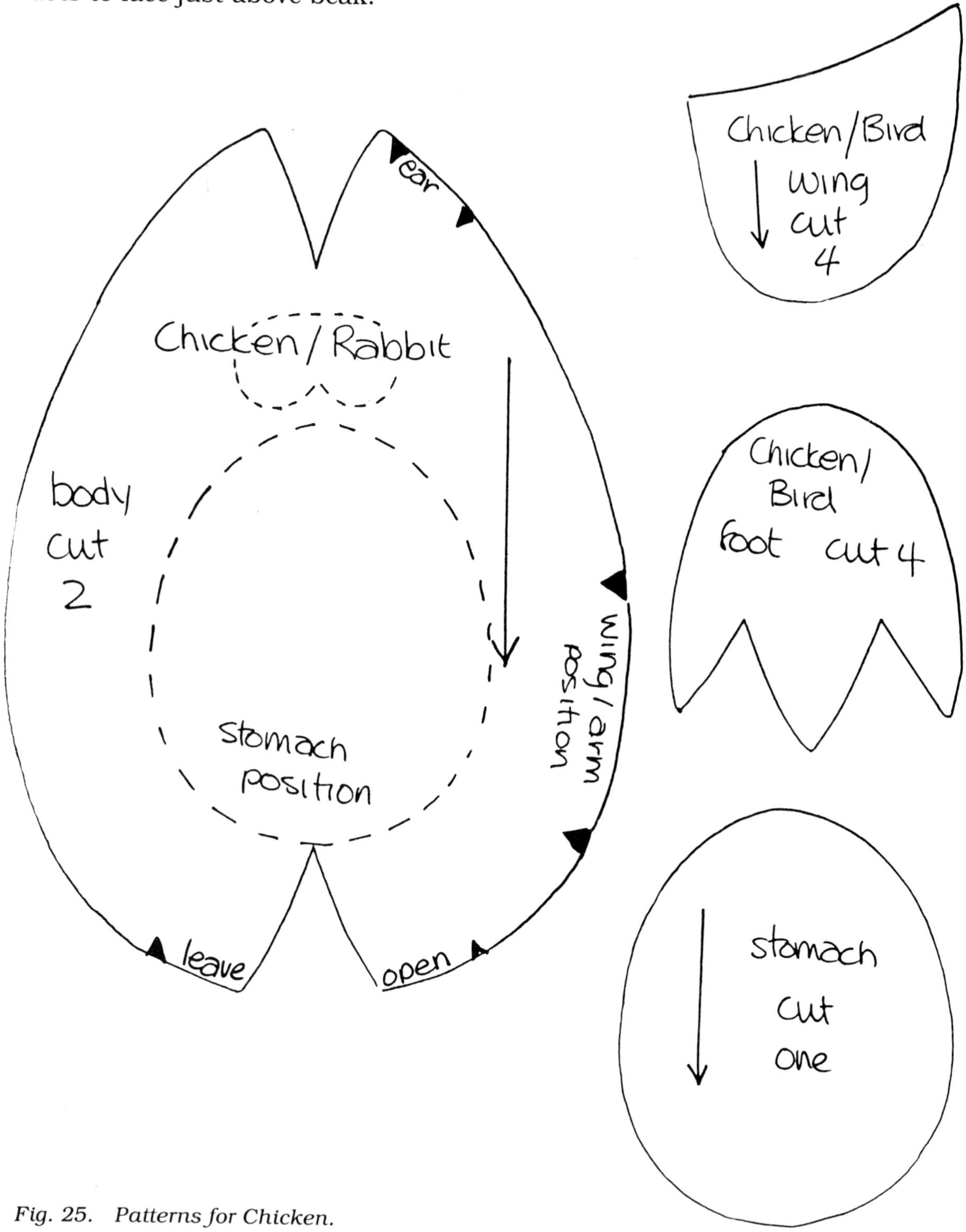

Chicken/Bird wing cut 4

Chicken/Rabbit

ear

body cut 2

stomach position

wing/arm position

leave

open

Chicken/ Bird foot cut 4

stomach cut one

Fig. 25.   Patterns for Chicken.

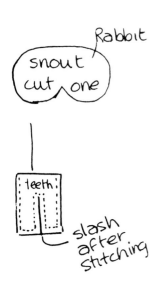

Fig. 26. Ear lining, snout, and teeth patterns for Rabbit. More patterns can be found on pages 29 and 30.

RABBIT:

Material: *12 x 12" tan fur for body*
2 x 5" white fur for stomach, tail, snout
scraps of pink fur for ear linings, nose
scraps of pink, black, white, and green felt
for eyes, teeth, carrot greens
2½ x 2½" orange felt for carrot
1 x 2" small check gingham (pink) for bow
1 oz. stuffing

Make ears by stitching together in pairs, right sides facing, leaving open at bottom. Turn. Stick ear linings in place on front of ears and topstitch all around edge of linings, through all thicknesses. Set aside.

Stitch arms together in pairs, right sides facing, leaving top open. Turn and stuff lightly. Close with a line of machine stitching. Stitch teeth along dotted line indicated and slash between teeth. Glue teeth to snout so they protrude below. Sew body darts.

Stick snout in place on body front and topstitch all around close to edge, catching top edge of teeth in stitching. Apply stomach as described for snout. Baste ears and arms in position on body front, so they point forward. Right sides facing, sew body front and back together, catching arms and ears in stitching and leaving bottom open. Turn and stuff. Close bottom by hand.

Stitch dart on foot top. Sew foot top to sole, right sides facing, leaving open at heel. Turn and stuff firmly. Close opening by hand and sew feet to bottom of body.

Make nose by basic circle method. Stitch to top of snout. Stick eyes with black pupil, pink iris, and white to face.

Make bow by folding gingham into 1" square and stitching around 3 open sides, leaving small opening to turn through. Turn and stitch closed. Gather center to form bow and stitch to front of rabbit.

Right sides facing, fold carrot along dotted line and stitch from wide end to point, leaving curved edge open. Turn and stuff. Slash along lines on carrot green and roll up to form fringe. Gather top of carrot piece and insert green fringe into opening. Stitch securely. Carrot may be stitched to rabbit's hand if desired.

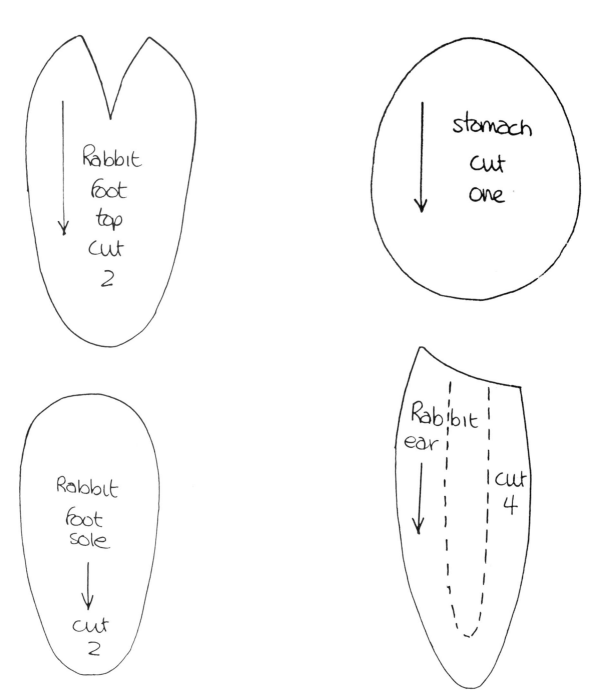

Fig. 27. Foot, stomach, and ear patterns for Rabbit. Use the body pattern on page 27 for Rabbit.

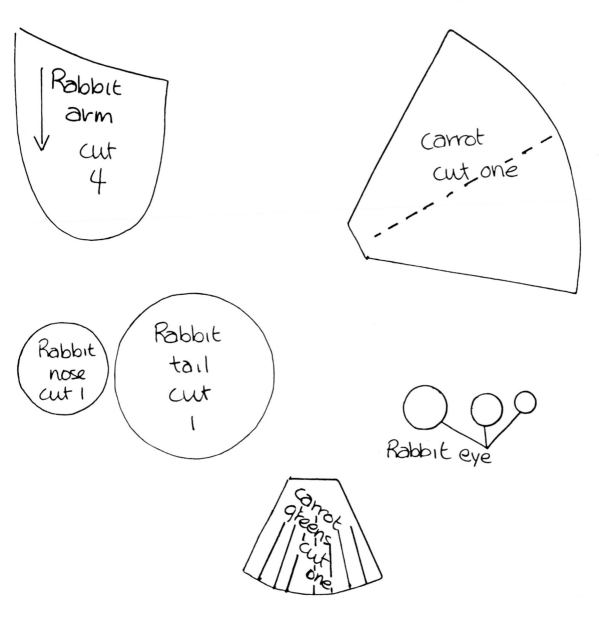

Fig. 28. More patterns for Rabbit.

BLUEBIRD:

Material: *Materials as for chicken, substituting blue for yellow fur.*

Make bluebird exactly as for chicken. See pages 26 and 27 for patterns.

Mother and Baby Chickens

Fig. 29.   Mother Chicken flanked by Baby Chickens.

Material: *12 x 18″ yellow fur for Mother Chicken*
7 x 10″ each pink and blue fur for Baby Chickens
5½ x 7″ red felt for comb, wattles
9 x 10″ orange felt for beaks, feet
8 oz. stuffing
paste-on moving eyes, 1 pair 15 mm; 2 pair 7 mm

Mother and Baby Chickens are made the same way, omitting comb and wattles for Baby Chickens.

BODY: Sew darts in head pieces. Right sides facing, sew gusset to one side of body from A-B. Sew second body piece to first, matching A, B, and head darts, and leaving open as indicated. Turn right-side out and stuff firmly. Close by hand.

FEET: Place together in pairs, wrong sides facing, and fasten with glue. Topstitch close to edge with matching thread all around. For Baby Chicken, you might want to do this by hand. Glue feet in place, splayed out from beneath chicken. Stitch to hold secure.

BEAK: Stitch together, right sides facing, 2 upper beak pieces along notched edge. Now, with wrong sides facing, stitch upper beak to lower beak close to edge all around, matching points and leaving top open. Stuff firmly, being careful to retain point. Gather slightly to close and attach to face with glue and stitching.

WINGS: Stitch together in pairs, right sides facing, leaving straight edge open. Turn but do not stuff. Close with whip stitch, pulling up slightly on thread. Attach to body where indicated on pattern.

EYES: Glue in place on face, just above beak.

COMB: (Mother only) Glue comb pieces together, wrong sides facing, and topstitch all around close to edge. Sew to head of mother with high curl to front.

WATTLES: (Mother only) Fold wattle piece in half along dotted line and apply to mother's face just below beak, using glue and firm stitches.

Fig. 30. Beak patterns for Mother Chicken. More patterns can be found on pages 33 to 36.

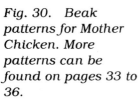

Mother Chicken upper beak cut 2

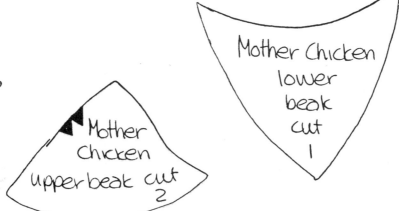

Mother Chicken lower beak cut 1

Here is just a sample of the many toys that can be created
through the circle method described in Chapter 2. Shown from
top to bottom are: Duck, Spider, Mouse, Pumpkin, Snowman,
Cat, Dog, Beaver, Bee, Lady Bug, Frog, and Pumpkin (again).
Using your imagination, you can create many more variations.

After mastering circle designs, the next step is simple shapes (Chapter 3). In top row are Lady Bug Pillow, MacTavish Dog (with tam) and two other Dogs. In middle row are Mother Chicken with Babies, Mice, and Gooney Birds. Bottom row shows Rabbit, different varieties of Birds, and more Mice!

Rabbits and Bears make irresistible toys. Chapter 4 shows how to make many of these Rabbits and Bears, including the pair of Tiny Bears, the Bears with Vests, and both the brown and pink Rabbits.

D

Beards add a wonderful new dimension to stuffed toys. In
Chapter 6 you will discover patterns and instructions for making
these two characters: Hamish MacSporran, splendidly
distinctive in his tartan, orange beard, and tam; and the Viking,
complete with helmet, belt buckle, and boot laces.

Christmas decorations (opposite page) always add a special
touch to the holiday season. Chapter 7 shows how to make
Ornaments, Finger Puppets, and, of course, those two classics—
Santa and the Elf.

Lion and Tiger (Chapter 8) in their "habitat." The Sasquatch and Monkey were added to give more authenticity to the jungle scene.

(Opposite page) These dolls (Chapter 5) have removable clothing, comb-able hair, and bendable limbs and range in personalities from the Witch and Angel in the back row to the two "laid-back" Teenagers and the Springtime Fairy in the first row. The Black Cat belongs to the Witch.

Author Jennifer MacLennan with just a few of her friends. This intimate group includes Rabbits, Bears, Lions, and Tigers—children's favorites.

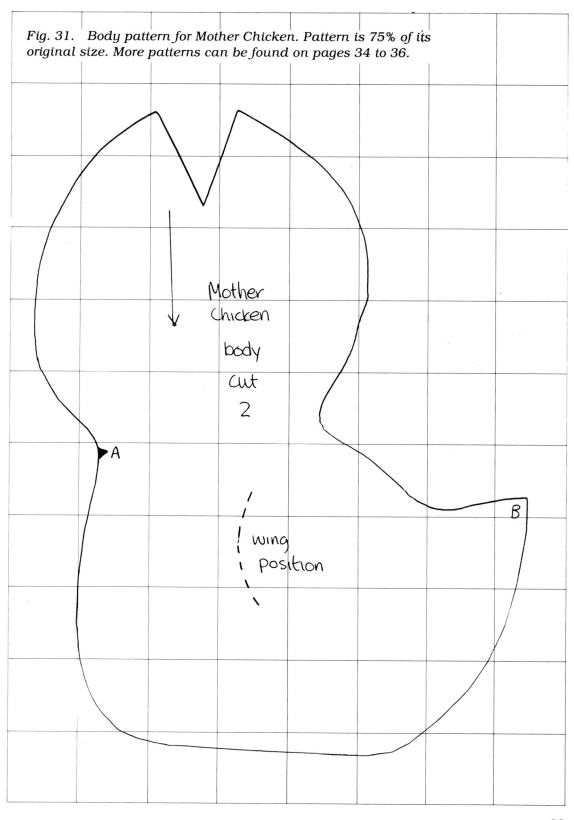

Fig. 31. Body pattern for Mother Chicken. Pattern is 75% of its original size. More patterns can be found on pages 34 to 36.

Mother
Chicken
body
Cut
2

A

B

wing
position

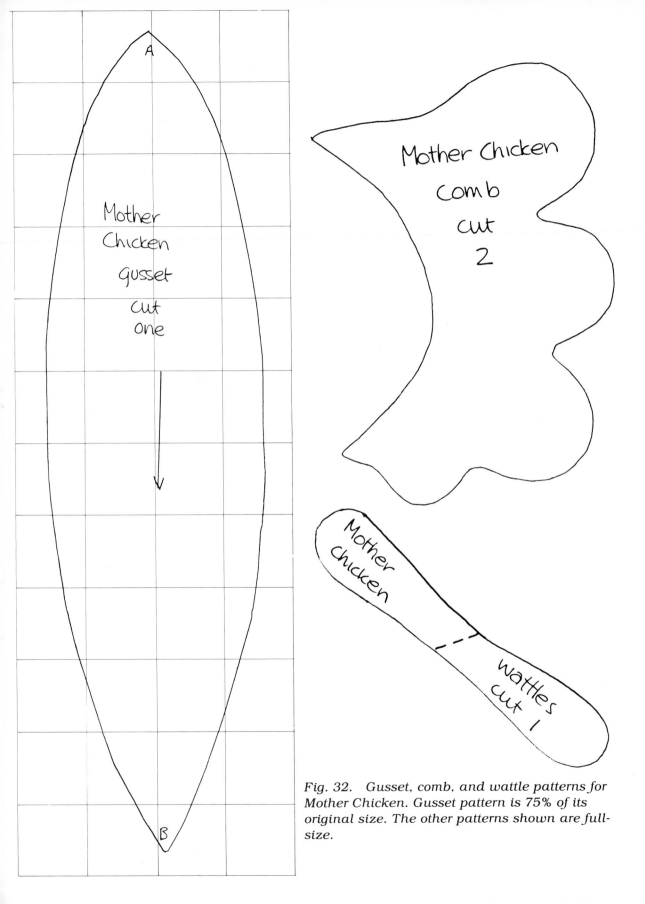

Mother Chicken gusset cut one

A

B

Mother Chicken comb cut 2

Mother Chicken wattles cut 1

Fig. 32. Gusset, comb, and wattle patterns for Mother Chicken. Gusset pattern is 75% of its original size. The other patterns shown are full-size.

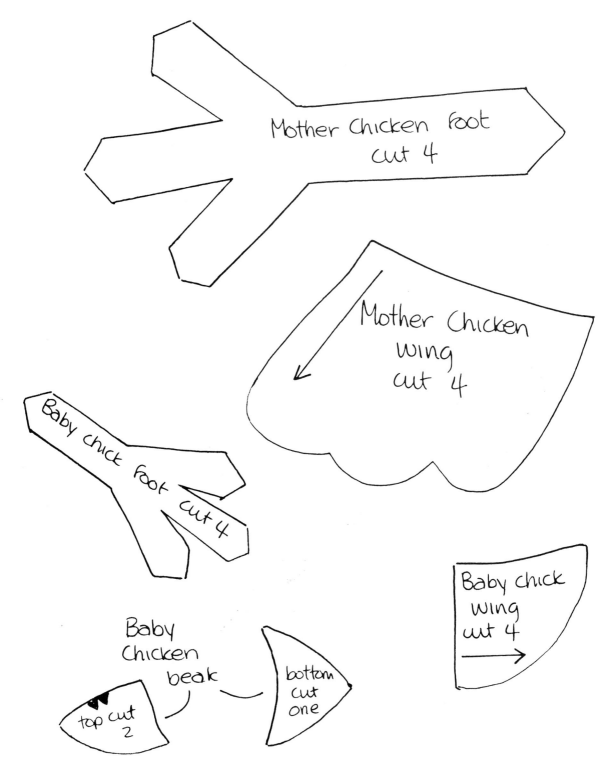

Mother Chicken Foot
cut 4

Mother Chicken
wing
cut 4

Baby chick foot cut 4

Baby chick
wing
cut 4

Baby
Chicken
beak

bottom
cut
one

top cut
2

Fig. 33.   Foot and wing patterns for Mother Chicken. Also beak, wing, and foot patterns for Baby Chickens. More patterns can be found on page 36.

35

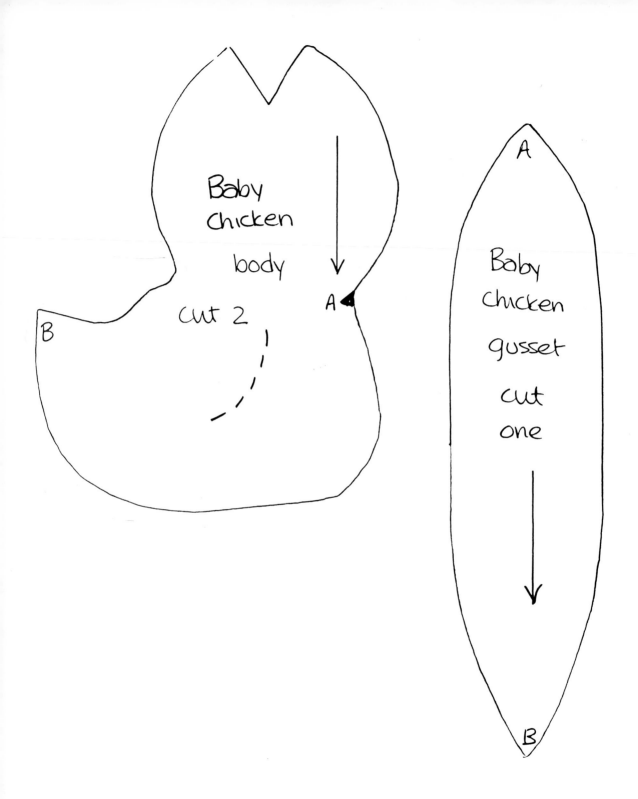

Baby
Chicken
body

Cut 2

A

B

Baby
Chicken
gusset

cut
one

A

B

Fig. 34.   Body and gusset patterns for Baby Chickens.

MacTavish Dog

Fig. 35. MacTavish Dog makes an adorable and faithful pet.

Material: *6 x 8" white fur for body*
scrap of black fur for ears
scraps of black felt for eye patches, nose, tail
½ oz. stuffing
2" circle for tam (see color page B)
1 pair moving eyes, 10 mm

Right sides facing, sew nose dart. Insert ears, fur side up, into slash in head back. Stitch slash so ear is caught in stitching. Matching A-B, stitch underbody to one side of body around legs, right sides facing. Matching all edges, right sides facing, stitch second body side to first side and gusset, leaving open at bottom. Turn right-side out and stuff firmly. Close by hand. Glue nose and eye patches in place. Glue eyes over patches. Glue tail to rear of dog.

Make tam by circle method, but stuff only lightly. Attach to dog's head at angle. Finish with dot of felt in a coordinating color for button on tam.

Mac-
Tavish
ear
cut
2

Fig. 36. Ear pattern for MacTavish Dog. More patterns can be found on page 38.

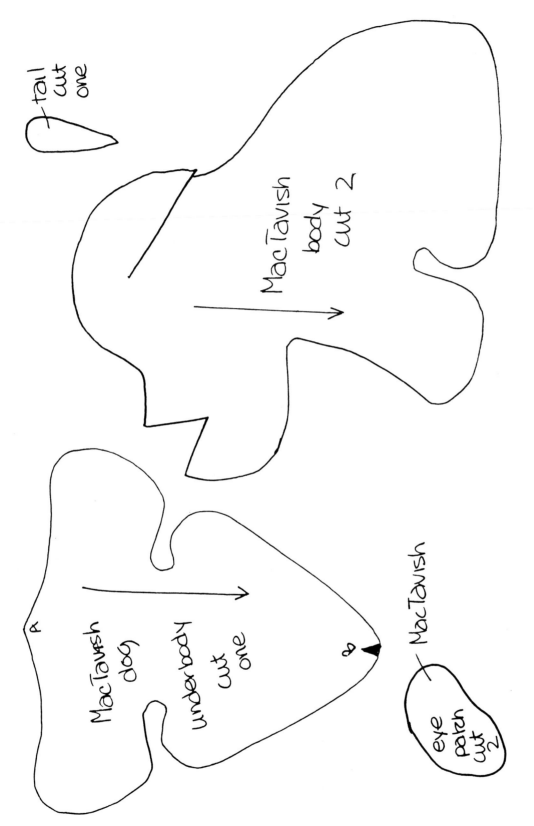

tail
cut
one

MacTavish
body
cut 2

MacTavish
dog

under body
cut
one

A

MacTavish

eye
patch
cut
2

Fig. 37. Patterns for MacTavish Dog.

4 Bears and Rabbits

Of all soft toys for children, bears and rabbits are probably the most popular. The toys in this chapter are basically anthropomorphic, or people-shaped, and all of them have personalities of their own. Most are made by similar techniques.

Before proceeding, refer once again to techniques in Chapter 1.

Herbert Hoppmann

Fig. 38. Herbert Hoppman (right) and Ernie Rabbit. Instructions for making Ernie Rabbit can be found on page 45.

Herb
paw
cut 4

Herb Hoppmann ear lining cut 2

Fig. 39. Paw and ear lining patterns for Herb Hoppman. More patterns can be found on pages 41 to 45.

Material: *18 x 30" (4 yd.) brown fur for body*
10 x 10" white fur for stomach, snout, pads
scraps of pink fur for nose, ear linings
scraps of white, pink, black felt for teeth, eyes
8 oz. stuffing

EARS: Stitch together in pairs, right sides facing. Leave bottom open. Turn right-side out but do not stuff. Glue ear linings to ears. Topstitch around edge of linings, through all thicknesses. Set aside.

ARMS: Place paw pads in place as marked on front of arms. Use opposite arm pieces (one right and one left), as you're working in pairs. Secure pads with a dab of adhesive and topstitch in position by hand or machine. Stitch back and front arm pieces together, right sides facing, leaving top open. Turn right-side out and stuff to within 1" of top. Close with a line of stitching. Set aside.

LEGS: Attach foot pads to soles as described for paws. Stitch legs together in pairs, right sides facing, leaving open top and bottom. Right sides facing, stitch soles to leg bottoms, matching notches to seam lines. Turn right-side out and stuff as for arms. Bring center seams together so that feet point forward. Close with a line of stitching. Set aside.

BODY: Sew all darts on body pieces and stomach piece. Apply stomach to body front as described for paw pads. Set aside. Glue together teeth pieces. Topstitch, following lines on pattern, and slash between teeth. Fasten to face with glue. Glue snout in position, overlapping teeth. Topstitch around edge, catching teeth in stitching. Pin and baste ears, arms, and legs, facing front, in place on front body. Stitch body front to body back, right sides facing, around edges, leaving bottom open and catching arms and ears in stitching. Turn. Stuff body firmly, filling cheeks carefully. Close bottom by hand.

FACE: Make nose by basic circle method, and glue and stitch in place. Cut out eyes in black, pink, and white felt. Glue pupils to pink and pink to whites. Glue in place on face.

TAIL: Make by basic circle method and attach to rear of body.

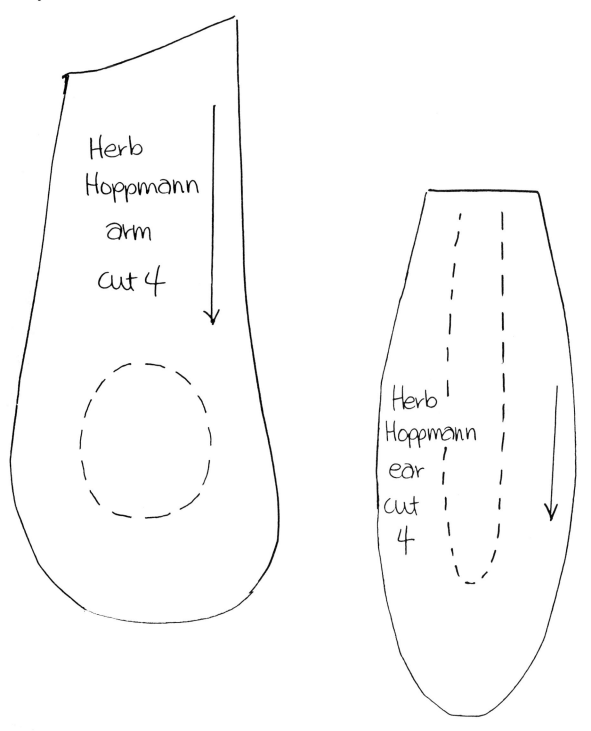

Fig. 40. Arm and ear patterns for Herbert Hoppman.

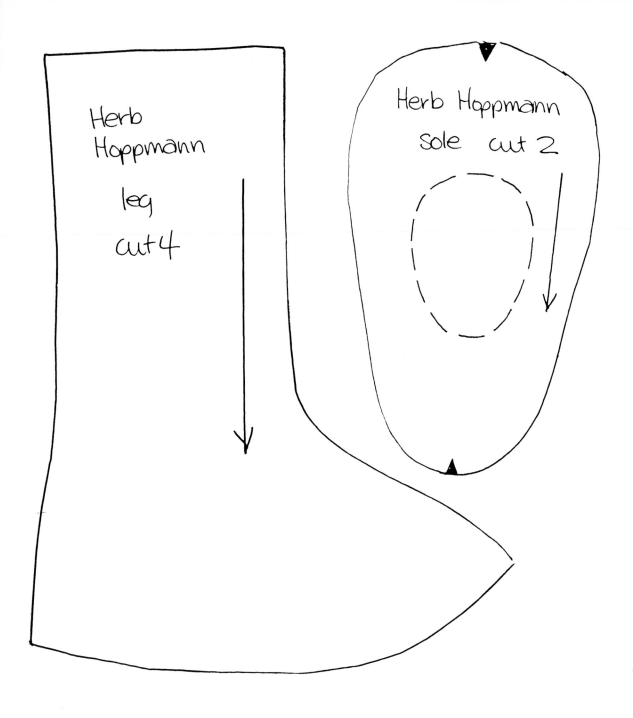

Herb
Hoppmann

leg

cut 4

Herb Hoppmann
Sole cut 2

Fig. 41. Leg and sole patterns for Herbert Hoppman.

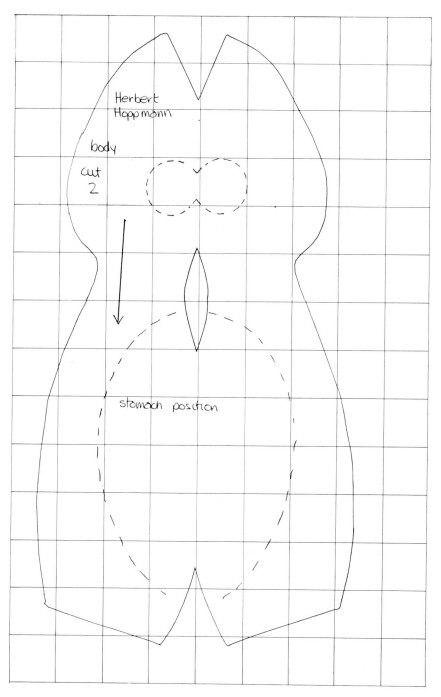

Herbert
Hoppmann

body

cut
2

stomach position

*Fig. 42. Body pattern for Herbert Hoppman. This pattern is 50%
of its original size. See pages 44 and 45 for more patterns.*

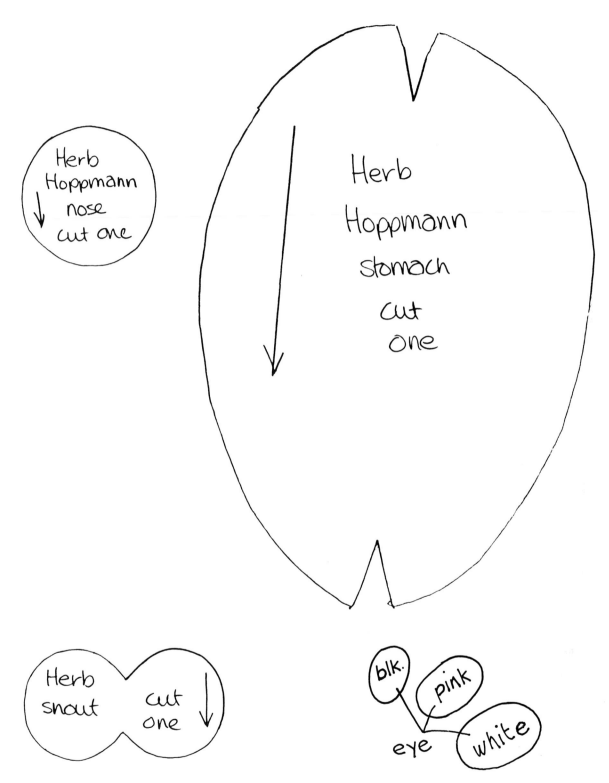

Fig. 43.   Stomach, snout, eye, and nose patterns for Herbert Hoppman.

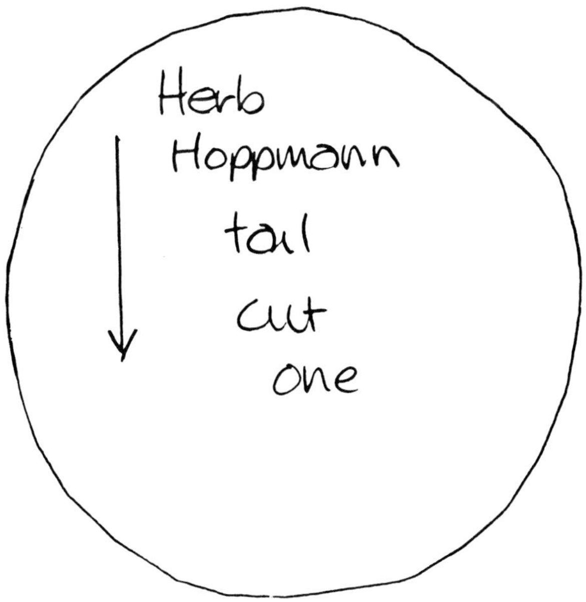

Fig. 44. Tail pattern for Herbert Hoppman.

Herb
Hoppmann
tail
cut
one

Ernie Rabbit

Material: 1/4 yd. white fur for body
5 x 3" white medium-pile fur for cheeks
5 x 6" pink fur for stomach, nose, ear linings
5 x 6" pink felt for paw pads
scraps of white and black felt for teeth and
    eyes
8 oz. stuffing

EARS: Stitch together in pairs, right sides facing, leaving bottoms open. Turn right-side out but do not stuff. Glue ear linings in place on ears. Topstitch around edge of linings, through all thicknesses. Set aside.

ARMS: Place paw pads in place as marked on fronts of arms. Use opposite arm pieces (one right and one left) as you're working in pairs. Secure pads with a dab of glue and topstitch in position by hand or machine. Place back and fronts together, right sides facing; stitch around arm, leaving top open. Turn right-side out and stuff firmly, filling to within 1" of top. Close with line of stitching.

LEGS: Attach foot pads to sole pieces as described for arms. Stitch legs together in pairs, right sides facing, leaving open at top and bottom. Right sides facing, stitch soles into bottom leg opening, matching notches A-B to seam lines as indicated. Turn right-side out and stuff to within 1″ of top. Bring center seams together so that feet point forward. Close with a line of stitching. Set aside.

BODY FRONT: Topstitch cheek pieces, close to edge all around, in place as marked on body. Sew stomach pieces to body fronts, matching H-J. Stitch body fronts together, right sides facing along G-H-J. Stitch head gusset into place, matching F-G-F. Baste arms, facing front in place on body front. Baste ears in position, also facing front, and stitch legs, so that feet face forward, to bottom edge of body front.

BODY BACK: Stitch together from C-D. Stitch body back to front, right sides facing, around edges, leaving bottom open and catching arms and ears in seam line. Turn upper part of body right-side out. Bring center back seam line together around legs and stitch K-E. Fold flat, front and back facing with legs protruding from back opening and stitch bottom seam, catching legs in stitching line. Pull legs through back opening to turn right-side out, and stuff body firmly, filling cheeks and shoulders carefully. Close up by hand.

TEETH: Sew 2 layers of felt together, close to edge as indicated by stitching lines on pattern. Slash center line. Stitch in place on front of face.

SNOUT: Make by basic circle method. Glue and stitch to face. Repeat for second snout piece.

NOSE: Make as for snout.

EYES: Cut out large and small pieces in black, middles in white. Glue in layers together as shown on pattern, and take a stitch through all 3 with white thread to give highlights. Glue in position on face.

TAIL: Make by circle method, and sew in place on back body.

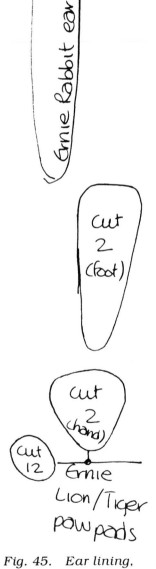

Fig. 45. Ear lining, foot, and paw pad patterns for Ernie Rabbit. More patterns can be found on pages 47 to 50.

46

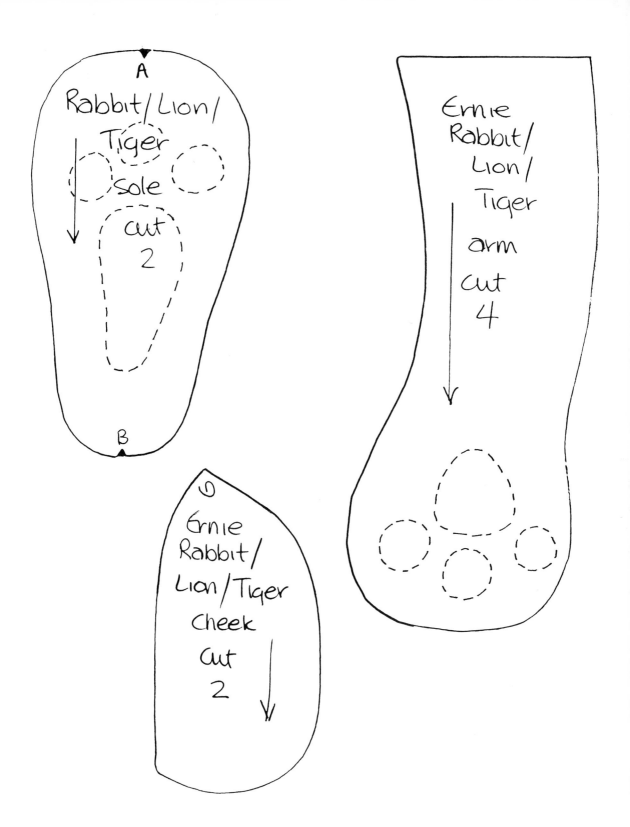

Fig. 46.   Cheek, sole, and arm patterns for Ernie Rabbit.

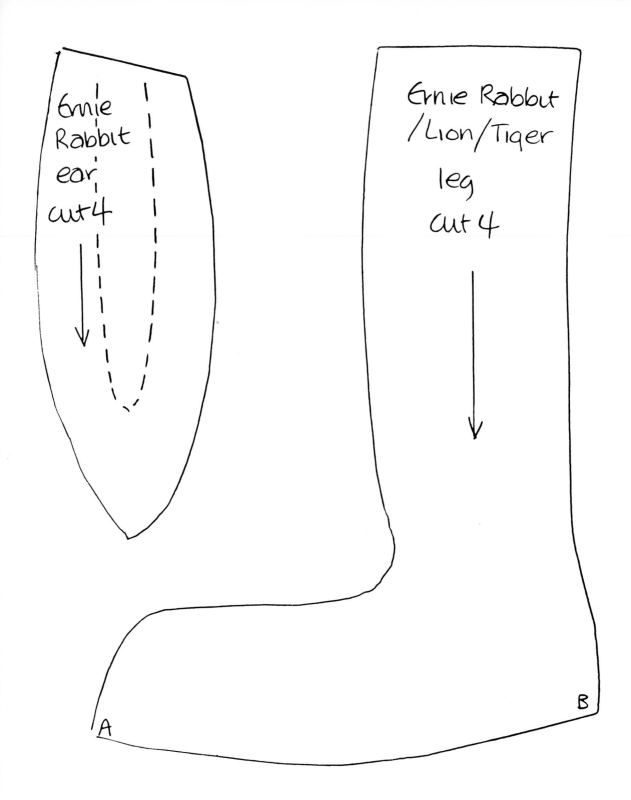

Fig. 47. Ear and leg patterns for Ernie Rabbit.

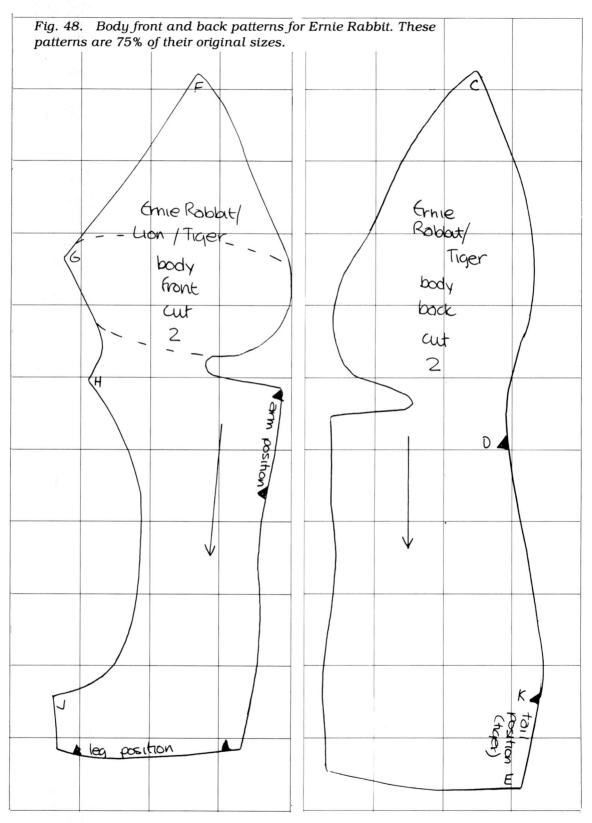

Fig. 48. Body front and back patterns for Ernie Rabbit. These patterns are 75% of their original sizes.

F

Ernie Rabbit/
Lion / Tiger
body
front
cut
2

G

H

arm position

leg position

J

C

Ernie
Rabbit/
Tiger
body
back
cut
2

D

K
tail
position
(tiger)
E

49

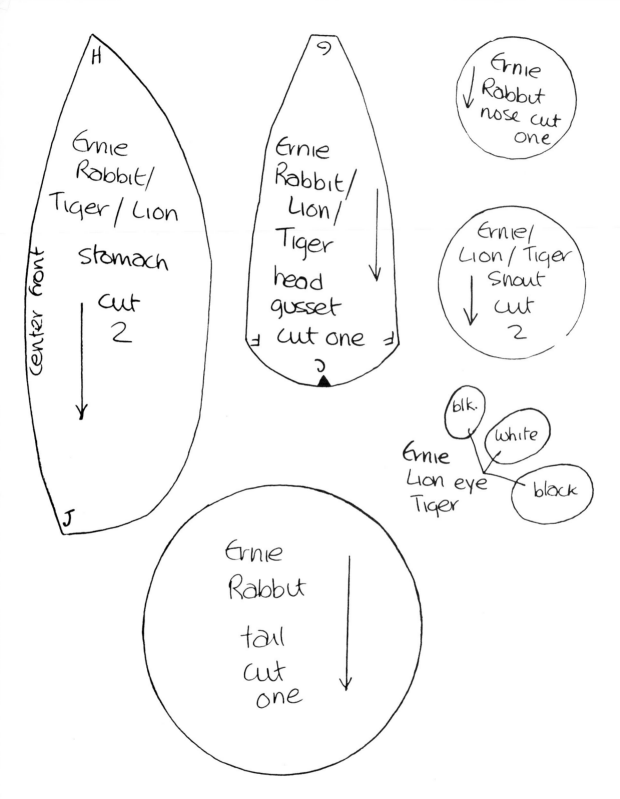

Fig. 49. Stomach, head gusset, nose, snout, eye, and tail patterns for Ernie Rabbit.

Bear with Vest

Fig. 50.   This dapper Bear is ready for work or play.

Material: ½ yd. fur for body
8 x 30" felt for vest, pads in coordinating
color
1 pair plastic lock-in eyes, 15 mm
1 yd. yarn
16 oz. stuffing

EARS: Stitch together in pairs, right sides together, leaving open at bottom. Turn but do not stuff. Close with a line of stitching. Set aside.

ARMS: Make as for Ernie Rabbit. Set aside.

LEGS: Make as for Ernie Rabbit. Set aside.

TAIL: Prepare as for ears. Set aside.

BODY BACK: Baste tail in position on center back seam of body. Stitch body back together along C-D.

FRONT: Baste and stitch body front from E-F. Stitch head gusset in place at G-E-G. Apply lock-in eyes as described in Chapter 1 (pages 7 and 8). Baste arms, facing front, in place on front body. Repeat for ears and legs. Stitch legs securely to body front. Right sides facing, sew body front to body back, matching all markings, and catching ears and arms in stitching. Leave bottom (where legs are attached) open. Turn right-side out and stuff firmly. Close bottom by hand.

SNOUT: Make flattened ball by circle method. Attach snout to face with ladder stitch. With black yarn, embroider nose and smiling mouth on snout.

VEST: Topstitch all edges of vest ⅛″ from edge. Fold and press lapels along fold line. Topstitch folded edge. Sew shoulder seams, right sides facing, catching lapels in stitching. Turn right-side out. Attach button to vest front where marked on pattern. Cut small slit for buttonhole and topstitch around edge. Put vest on bear.

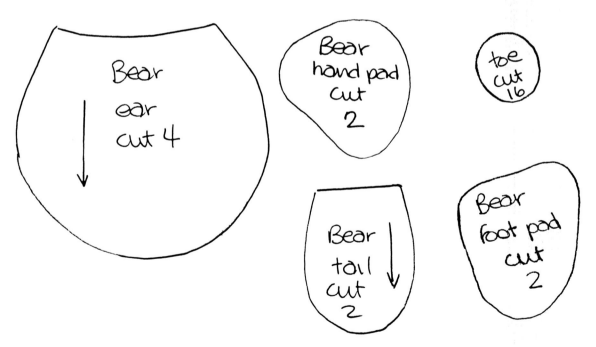

Fig. 51. Ear, hand pad, toe, tail, and foot pad patterns for Bear. More patterns appear on pages 53 to 58.

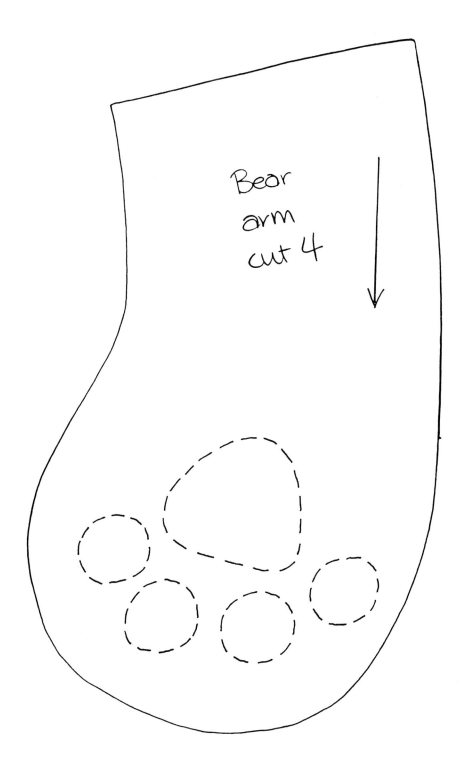

Fig. 52. Arm pattern for Bear.

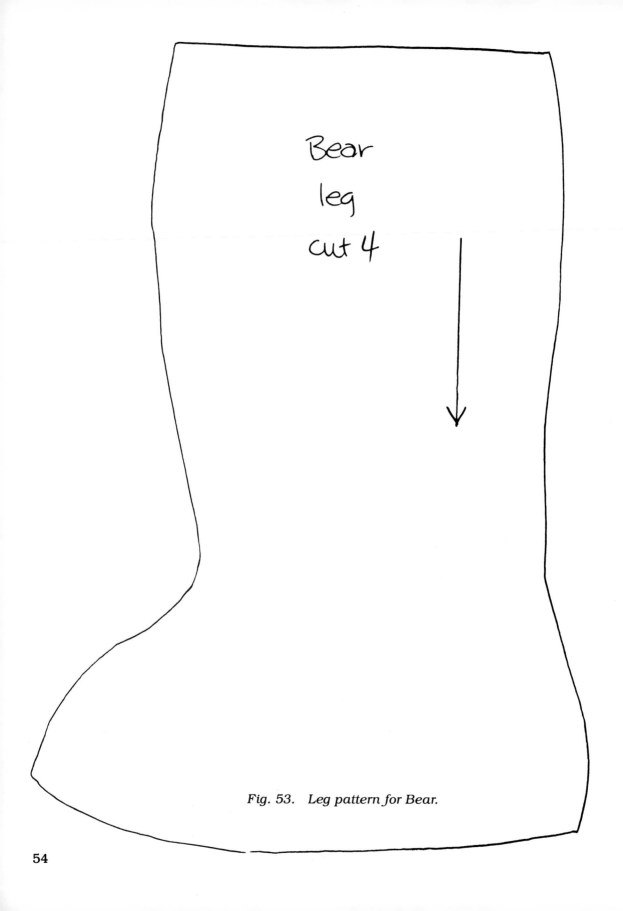

Bear

leg

cut 4

Fig. 53.   Leg pattern for Bear.

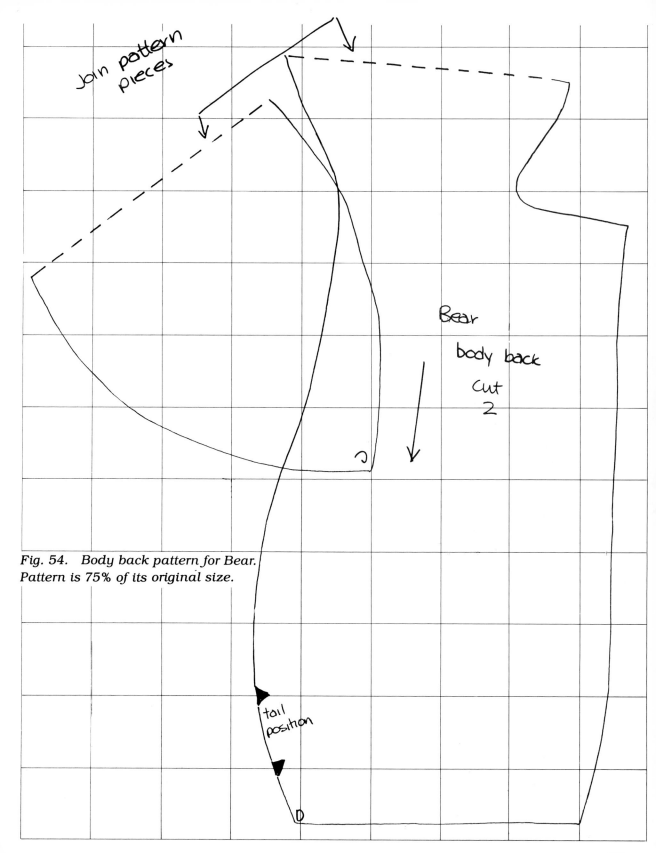

Join pattern pieces

Bear

body back

cut

2

Fig. 54. Body back pattern for Bear. Pattern is 75% of its original size.

tail position

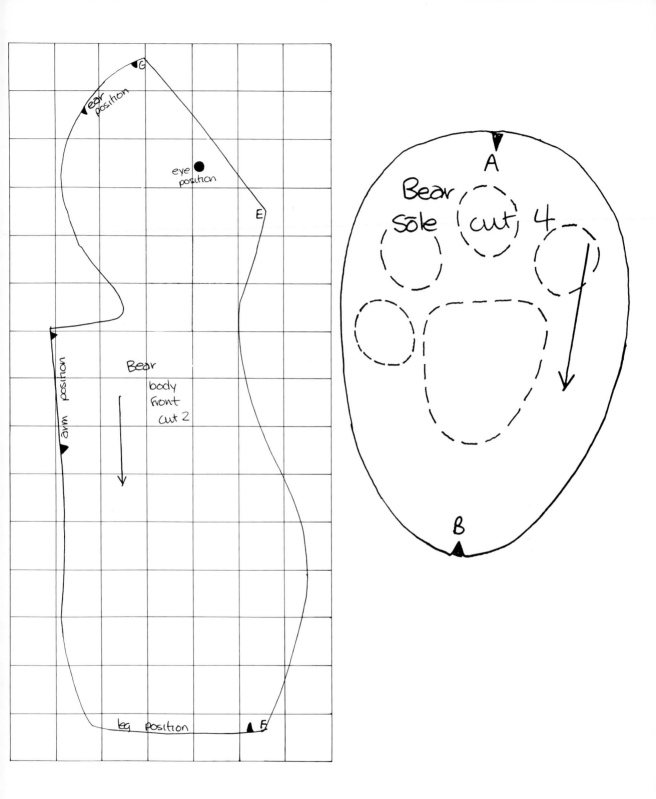

Within the body front pattern (left):
- G
- ear position
- eye position
- E
- arm position
- Bear body Front cut 2
- leg position
- F

Within the sole pattern (right):
- A
- Bear Sole (cut) 4
- B

Fig. 55. Body front and sole patterns for Bear. Body front pattern is 50% of its original size. Sole pattern is full-size.

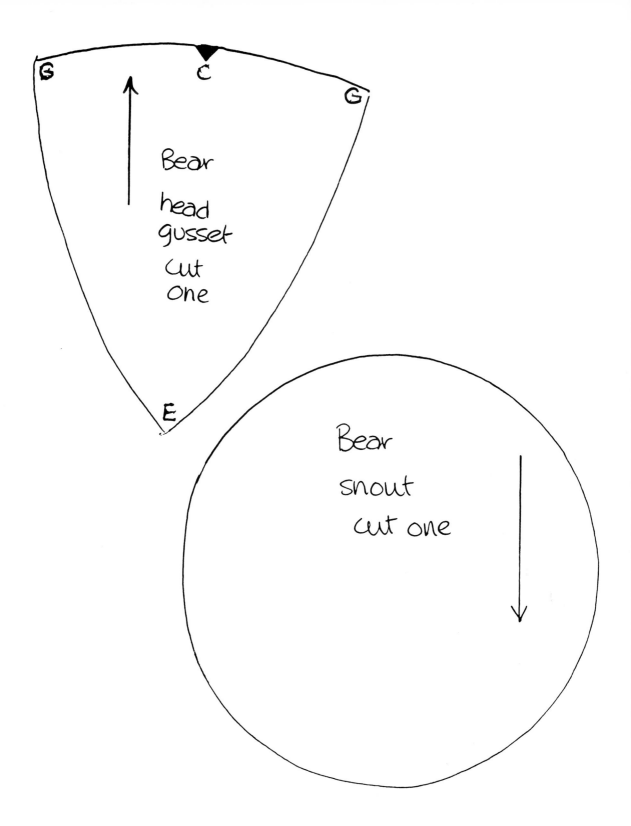

Fig. 56. Snout and head gusset patterns for Bear.

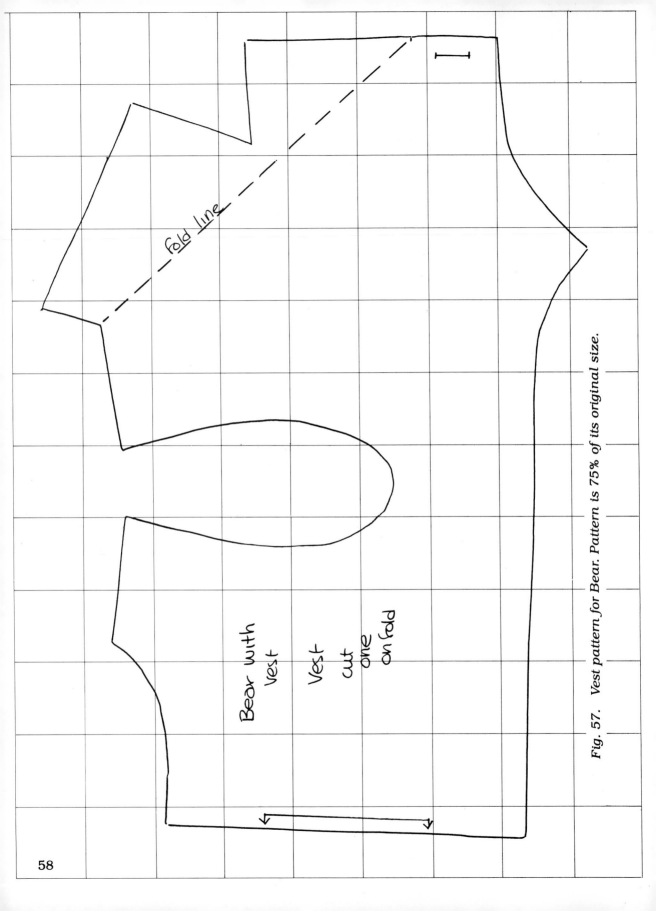

fold line

Bear with
vest

Vest
cut
one
on fold

Fig. 57. Vest pattern for Bear. Pattern is 75% of its original size.

Tiny Bears

Fig. 58. These two Tiny Bears can be a daughter and son complement to the fellow on page 51. The daughter is wearing a jumper decorated with a daisy; the son—clad in a vest—likes to dress like his father.

Material: 8 x 14" fur for body
4 x 10" coordinating felt for vest/jumper
1 pair lock-in plastic eyes, 10 mm
1 tiny button for vest front
scraps of white, yellow, and green felt for daisy
scrap of black felt for nose
1 oz. stuffing

EARS: Stitch together in pairs, right sides facing, around outer edge, leaving top open. Turn right-side out but do not stuff. Set aside.

TAIL: Fold in half so curved edges meet. Stitch around curved edge, leaving open at top. Turn. Set aside.

BODY FRONT: Right sides facing, stitch body center front seam X-A. Stitch head gusset to head matching Y-X-Y. Apply eyes as described in Chapter 1 (pages 7 and 8). Baste ears in position on body front.

BODY BACK: Right sides facing, stitch center back seam B-C. Baste tail to back body in position indicated on pattern. Stitch back body D-A, catching tail in seam line. Right sides facing, matching points A-B and all edges, stitch front and back together. Turn bear right-side out through back opening. Stuff arms and legs. Stitch across where indicated by dotted lines on pattern, to form hinges for limbs. Finish stuffing bear and close back by hand. Glue nose in position on snout.

FEET: Fold feet forward and hand stitch to secure in position.

VEST: Fold and press lapels to right side along line indicated on pattern. Right sides facing, sew shoulder seams. Turn right-side out and put on bear. Overlap left side of vest over right and stitch closed. Stitch button to front of vest.

JUMPER: Right sides facing, stitch shoulder seams. Turn right-side out and put on bear. Secure with a line of glue. Complete with daisy made as follows: Gather along straight edge and pull up tight. Secure at back with a stitch or two. Stick felt dot in middle for center of daisy. Glue flower and leaf shape to jumper front.

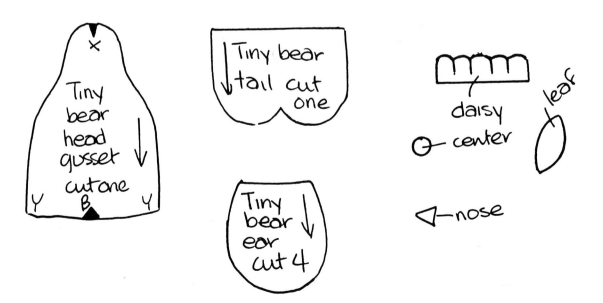

Fig. 59. Head gusset, tail, ear, nose, and daisy patterns for Tiny Bears. More patterns appear on pages 61 to 63.

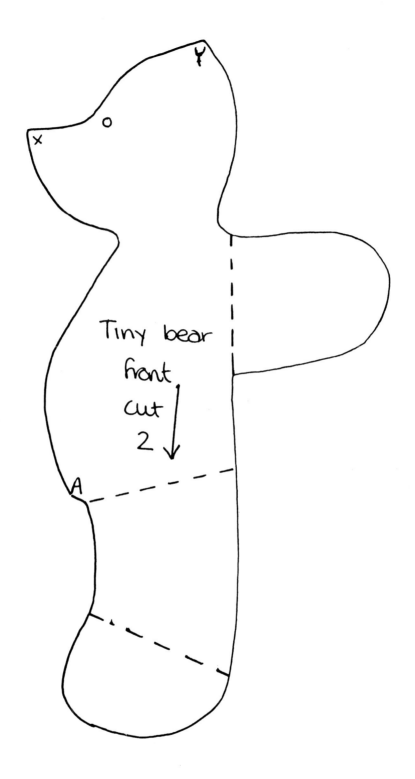

Fig. 60.   *Front pattern for Tiny Bears.*

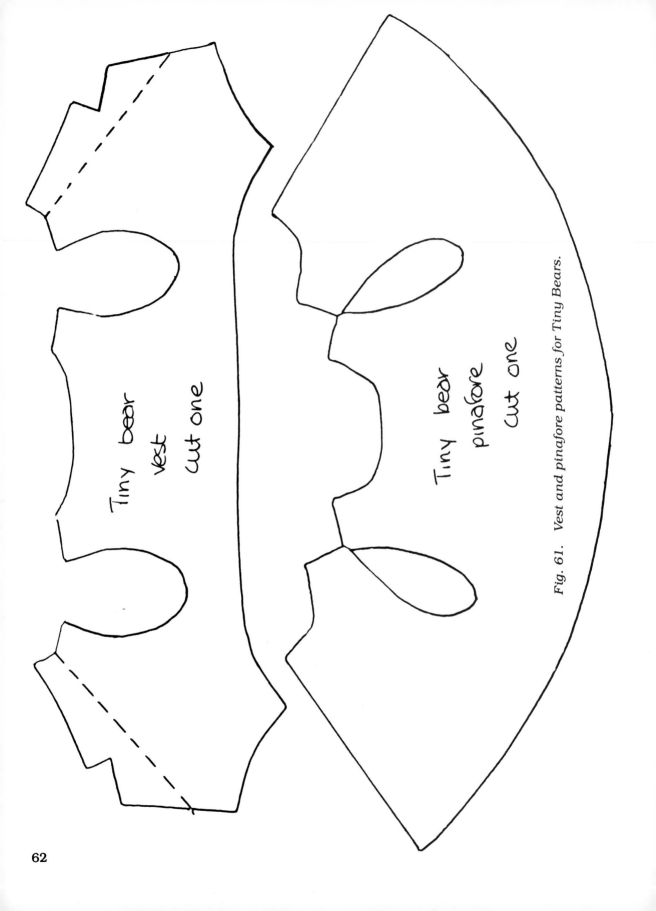

Tiny bear
vest
cut one

Tiny bear
pinafore
cut one

Fig. 61. Vest and pinafore patterns for Tiny Bears.

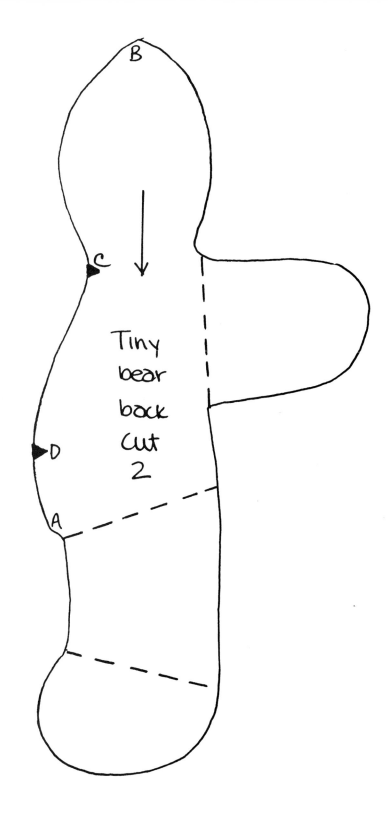

B

C

Tiny
bear
back
Cut
2

D

A

Fig. 62. Back pattern for Tiny Bears.

5 Dolls

Most young children love dolls, and I was no exception. All of the dolls here incorporate features young children love—removable clothing, bendable limbs, and comb-able hair. Some are made from similar patterns, and as a result they may have entire wardrobes based on each other's clothes.

Sonya and Sylvia

Fig. 63.   Sylvia and Sonya: two "laid-back" teenagers. While Sylvia prefers jeans and a sweatshirt, Sonya is more comfortable in a dress.

Material: *(amounts listed are enough for both dolls)*

24 x 36" cotton fabric or blend for bodies

3 x 6" each brown and yellow long-pile fur for wigs

9 x 12" cotton print for Sonya's dress

3 x 7" plain cotton for panties

6½ x 12" plain cotton for Sylvia's jeans

4½ x 7" each felt for Sonya's shoes, and Sylvia's sneakers

7 x 10" knit fabric for Sylvia's sweatshirt

4 x 7" rib knit for sweatshirt

3½" of ¼" thick elastic, 8" of ⅛" thick elastic

5 oz. stuffing

felt scraps for eyes, green and brown

pink thread for mouths

pink crayon for coloring cheeks

3 snap fasteners

narrow lace, 7"

Dolls

Intructions for both dolls are the same.

ARMS: Stitch together in pairs, right sides facing, all around leaving top open. Turn right-side out and stuff to within ¾" of top. Set aside.

LEGS: Stitch together in pairs, right sides facing, leaving open at top and bottom. Sew sole to bottom of foot, matching notches A-B to center front and back seams. Turn right-side out and stuff to within ¾" of top. Set aside.

BODY: Place together in pairs, right sides facing, and stitch along center seam C-D. Open out flat. Baste and sew legs to bottom of body front, so that feet point forward. Baste arms in position on body front. Place front and back body pieces together, right sides facing, and sew all around, leaving bottom open and catching arms in stitching line. Turn and stuff firmly, filling cheeks and shoulders carefully. Close bottom seam by hand.

Fig. 64. Eye, sole, and shoe sole patterns for Sylvia and Sonya. More patterns appear on pages 66 to 69.

FACE: Embroider smiling mouth in place. Color cheeks with pink crayon. Glue eye dots on face.

WIG: Right sides facing, sew darts on wig side. Matching dart seam, right sides facing, stitch together along top of wig, E-F, being careful not to catch pile in stitching. Turn right-side out and stick on doll. Glue in place and hand sew around edge. Comb or brush to neaten.

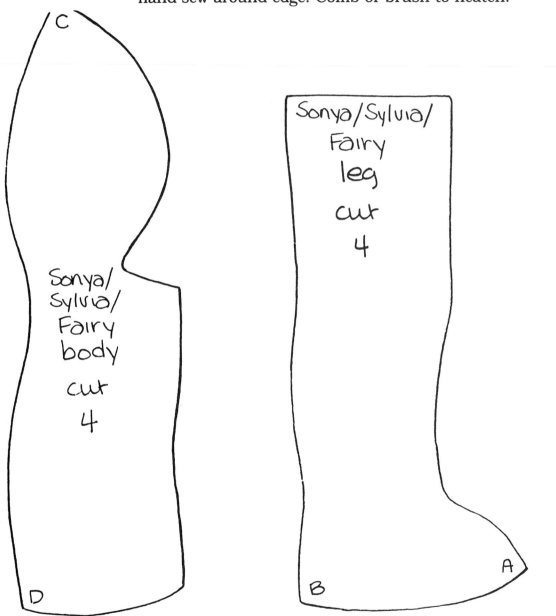

C

Sonya/ Sylvia/ Fairy body

cut 4

D

Sonya/Sylvia/ Fairy leg

cut 4

B

A

Fig. 65. Body and leg patterns for Sylvia and Sonya.

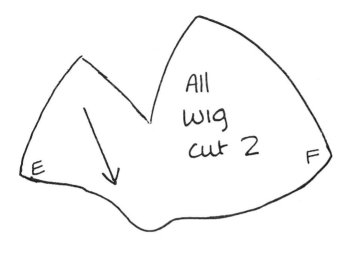

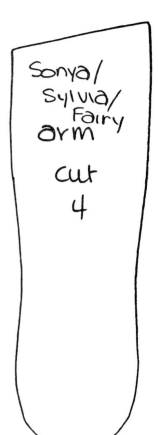

Fig. 66. Wig and arm patterns for Sylvia and Sonya.

Sonya's Clothes

SHOES: Topstitch along top edge and cut-out edges. Fold, right sides facing, so heels meet, and stitch seam. Sew soles into shoes, matching heel notch to heel seam. Turn and put on doll.

PANTIES: Hem with narrow hem along leg edges. Attach lace. Fold under ¼″ at waist edge. Cut ⅛″ elastic to fit waist. Sew elastic, stretching to fit, along waist edge. Fold panties, right sides facing so center back seams meet, and sew. Refold so that crotch seams meet. Sew. Turn right-side out and put on doll.

DRESS: Sew bodice front to bodice back pieces, right sides facing, along shoulder seams. Turn narrow hem along neck and back edges. Right sides facing, sew sleeves to armhole openings, matching notch to shoulder seams. Fold up ½″ along edge of sleeve. Cut two pieces ⅛″ elastic to fit arms. Stitch elastic, stretching to fit, to sleeve edge along line indicated on pattern. Fold bodice so side seams meet. Stitch along underarm from waist to sleeve edge. Turn bodice right-side out. Hem bottom edge of skirt piece. Hem side edges about halfway down from waist edge. Run a gathering thread along waist edge and pull up to fit bodice. Pin, baste, and stitch in place. Fold dress so that center back edges meet, and sew from hem edge to ¾" from waist. Sew 2 snap fasteners to back at waist and neck. Put dress on doll.

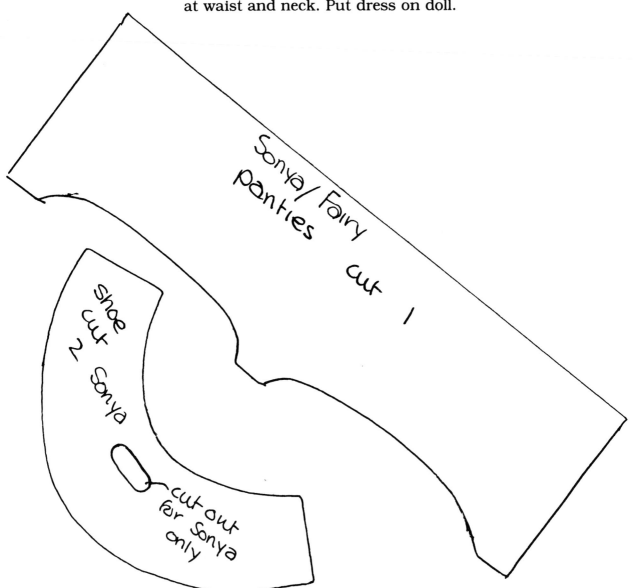

Fig. 67. *Shoe pattern for Sylvia and Sonya. Also, panties pattern for Sonya.*

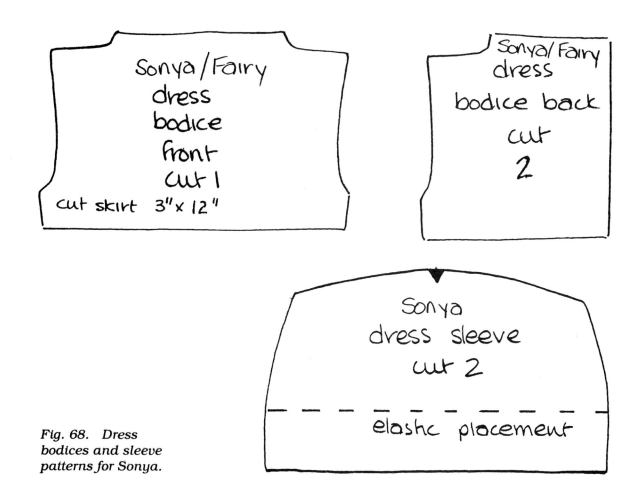

Fig. 68. Dress
bodices and sleeve
patterns for Sonya.

Sylvia's Clothes

SNEAKERS: Make as for Sonya's shoes, omitting top-stitching around cut-out (sneakers have no cut-out).

JEANS: Right sides facing, place together and sew center front crotch seam. Open out flat and stitch mock fly. Topstitch along line indicated on pattern, down center of each piece. Hem leg bottoms with narrow hem. Fold down ¼" at waist edge and apply ¼" elastic as described for panties. Stitch center back crotch seam. Fold so inseam edges meet and sew from leg hem to leg hem. Turn and press creases into pants. Put on doll.

SWEATSHIRT: Fold all bands in half lengthwise, wrong sides facing. Press. Stitch sleeve band to bottom of sleeve, matching raw edges, right sides facing, stretching to fit. Attach waist band in the same fashion. Fold down and press to form cuff. Sew sleeve to armhole opening, matching notch and edges. Sew shoulder and sleeve seams, from cuffs to neck. Attach neck band as for waist and cuffs. Hem back opening edges from neck down about 1½". Sew center back seam to hemmed edge. Turn and put snap fastener at neck. Place on doll.

HEADBAND: Fold in half lengthwise, right sides facing, and stitch. Turn right-side out and sew ends together to form loop. Put on doll.

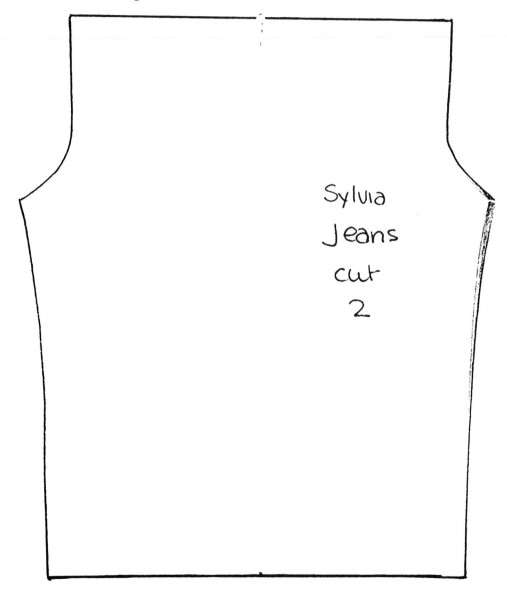

Sylvia
Jeans
cut
2

Fig. 69. Jeans pattern for Sylvia. For shoe and shoe sole patterns, see page 68. More clothes patterns appear on pages 71 and 72.

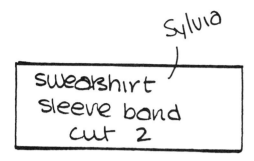

Sylvia
neckband   cut 1
Sweatshirt

Sylvia

Sweatshirt
sleeve band
cut 2

* for headband, cut
piece 3/4" x 5½" from
sweatshirt fabric

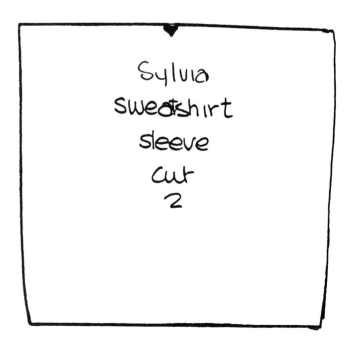

Sylvia
Sweatshirt
sleeve
cut
2

Fig. 70. Sweatshirt patterns for Sylvia.

Sylvia
Sweatshirt
cut
1

waistband
cut 1

sweatshirt

Sylvia

Fig. 71.   Sweatshirt patterns for Sylvia.

Springtime Fairy

Fig. 72. The favorite season for this jovial Fairy is springtime— when she surrounds herself with fields of bright, blossoming flowers.

Material: 18 x 24" cotton fabric or blend for body
3 x 6" frosted-green long-pile fur for hair
12 x 15" pale-yellow fabric for dress and panties
4½ x 7" green felt for shoes
3½" of ¼" thick elastic
20" green soutache braid
2½" oz. stuffing
scraps of white, pink, yellow, and green felt
pink thread for mouth
pink crayon for coloring cheeks
narrow lace, 7"
2 snap fasteners

DOLL: Make exactly as described for Sonya and Sylvia.
CLOTHES: Make shoes as described for Sylvia's sneakers, and top with a daisy made by the same technique described for the Tiny Bears in Chapter 4 (page 60). Pan-

73

ties are made as described for Sonya. Dress is also like Sonya's, except that skirt is longer and skirt edge and waist are trimmed with soutache braid, which is stitched on before sewing up back seam. Trim skirt with pink and white daisies. Butterfly is made like daisies, but with 4 petals instead of 5. Antennae are pieces of black thread. Make headband for fairy with a length of soutache braid trimmed with 3 daisies.

Patterns for the daisy can be found on page 60. Shoe pattern and panties pattern can be found on page 68. Dress patterns can be found on page 69.

Witch and Angel

Fig. 73. This nattily clad Witch is never without her black cat—a familiar.

Fig. 74. Traditional Angel complete with halo and wings.

WITCH:

Material: 16 x 18" green broadcloth for body

8 x 14" red/white dotted fabric for pantaloons

5 x 8" black long-pile fur for hair

8 x 12" black felt for hat, shoes, and cat ears

7 x 10" black velveteen for cat

scrap of yellow felt for buckle

8½" of ¼" thick elastic for waist of pantaloons

8" of ⅛" thick elastic for legs of pantaloons

1 pair 9 mm lock-in plastic eyes, green

16 x 18" black fabric for dress

2 snap fasteners

6 oz. stuffing

ANGEL:

Material: *16 x 18" flesh or pink fabric for body*
18 x 21" white fabric for dress/pantaloons
5 x 8" yellow or gold long-pile fur for hair
1 pair 9 mm lock-in plastic eyes, gold
6 x 7" yellow or gold felt for shoes
8½" gold cord for halo
1½ yd. gold rickrack, ¼" for trim
4½ x 6½" medium-weight non-woven
    interfacing for wings
2 snap fasteners
6 oz. stuffing

Dolls

Instructions for both dolls are the same.

ARMS: Right sides facing, stitch arms together all around edge, leaving top open. Turn right-side out and stuff, filling thumb carefully, to elbow. Bring center seams together, and stitch across at elbow. Continue stuffing to within 1" of top and close with a line of stitching. Set arms aside.

LEGS: Stitch legs together in pairs, right sides facing, leaving open at top and bottom. Matching notches to seam lines, stitch soles to bottom of feet, right sides facing. Turn. Fill as for arms, stitching across at knee. Set aside.

HEAD: Right sides facing, stitch head gusset to head sides, matching cheeks and leaving neck open. Turn right-side out and apply plastic eyes as described in Chapter 1 (pages 7 and 8). Stuff firmly, filling cheeks carefully. Set aside.

BODY: Baste arms and legs, facing front, in place on body front. Place front and back together, right sides facing, and stitch side seams, catching arms in stitching. Turn right-side out and stuff firmly. Close bottom by hand. Hand stitch head to neck, tucking in raw edges and adding more stuffing if needed to keep neck firm. Make nose by basic circle method. Position in place on face and stitch. Make mouth by embroidering smile in place with red thread.

Fig. 75. Foot sole and nose patterns for Witch and Angel. More patterns appear on pages 77 to 80.

HAIR: Make and apply to doll following directions for Sylvia.

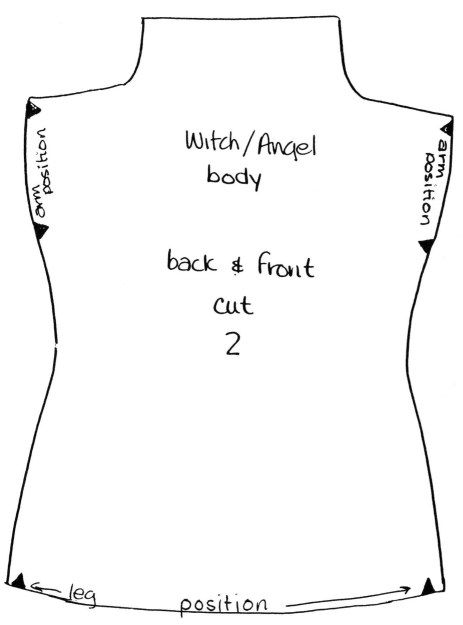

Fig. 76. *Body pattern for Witch and Angel.*

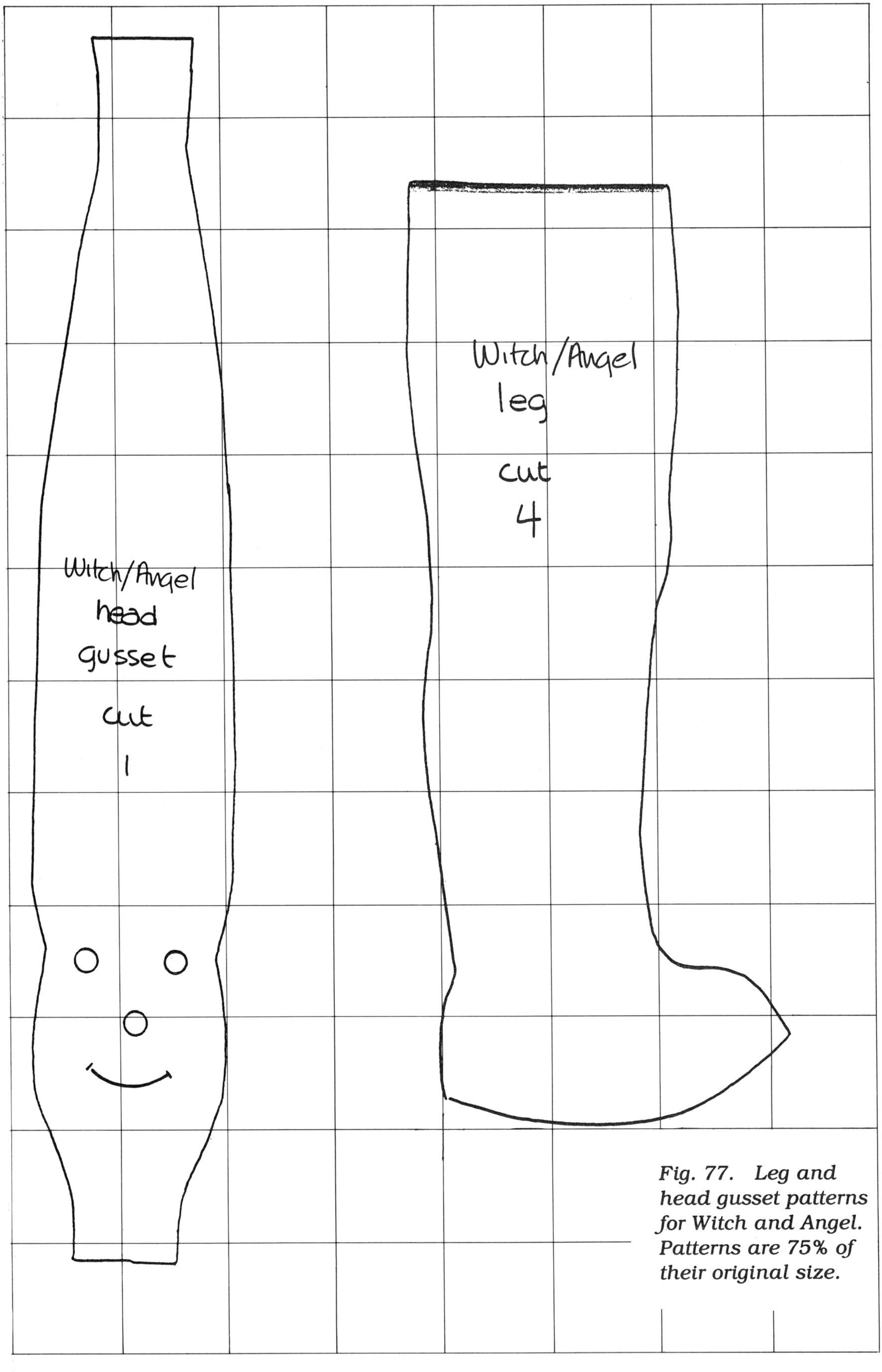

Witch/Angel
head
gusset

cut
1

Witch/Angel
leg

cut
4

Fig. 77. Leg and
head gusset patterns
for Witch and Angel.
Patterns are 75% of
their original size.

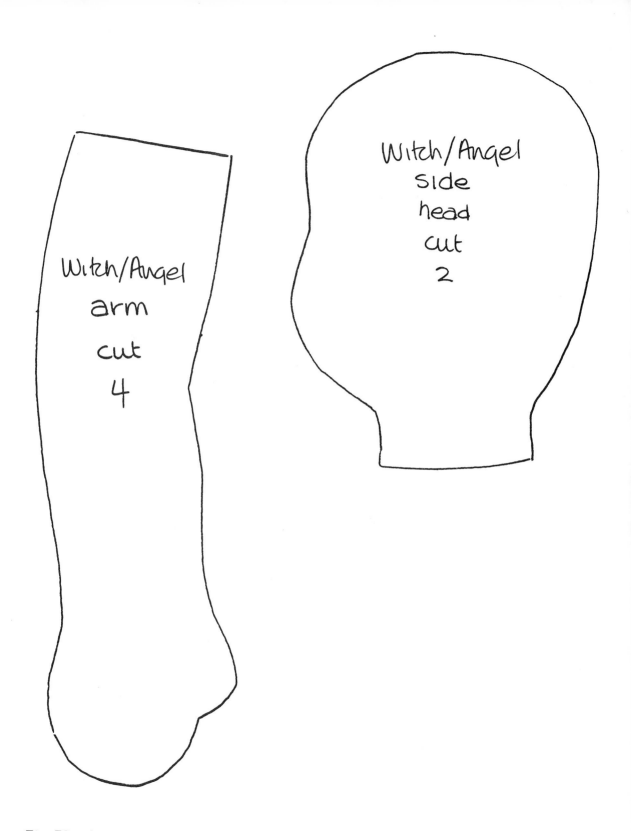

Witch/Angel
arm
cut
4

Witch/Angel
side
head
cut
2

Fig. 78. Arm and side head patterns for Witch and Angel.

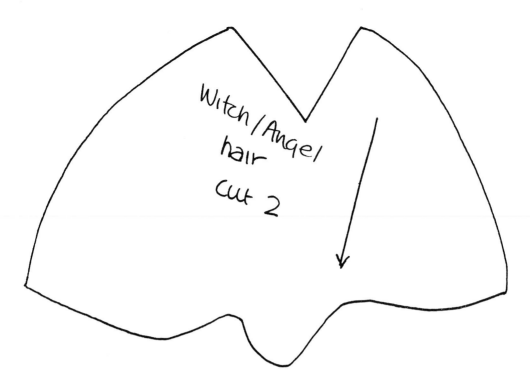

In the image: "Witch/Angel hair cut 2"

Fig. 79. Hair pattern for Witch and Angel.

WITCH'S CLOTHES

PANTALOONS: Right sides facing, stitch center front (C-F) seam from waist to crotch. Cut elastic to fit waist. Apply elastic to waistband by turning under ¼" to wrong side, and stitching elastic in place, stretching to fit. Turn up ½" of leg bottom and press. Cut elastic to fit leg. Apply elastic along leg bottom, leaving a grill protruding at edge. Right sides facing, sew center back (C-B). Stitch inseams from leg hem to leg hem and turn. Put on doll.

DRESS: Make as described for Sonya, omitting elastic on sleeve edge.

HAT: Iron interfacing to wrong side of hat piece. Right sides facing, fold into cone shape so points B meet. Sew seam A-B. Turn right-side out. Stitch brim with inner circle cut out to bottom of hat cone, right sides facing. Topstitch this brim, wrong sides facing, to second brim all around edges and tuck cut triangles inside hat. Stick down with glue. Make chin strap of elastic thread and sew to inside of hat. Glue buckle to front of hat and put on doll.

SHOES: Right sides facing, sew together in pairs along center front and back seams. Sew sole to bottom of shoe. Turn. Put on doll.

CAT: Right sides facing, sew head gusset to one side of cat head, matching A-B. Sew 2 cat bodies together from notch on front around head, back, and tail to notch in back. Right sides facing, stitch under body pieces together along upper curved edge, leaving open where indicated between notches. Sew underbody to body, matching seam lines. Turn and stuff carefully. Sew ears to head and embroider eyes and nose in place.

buckle
Cut
1
yellow
felt

Witch/Angel
shoe

Sole
cut
2

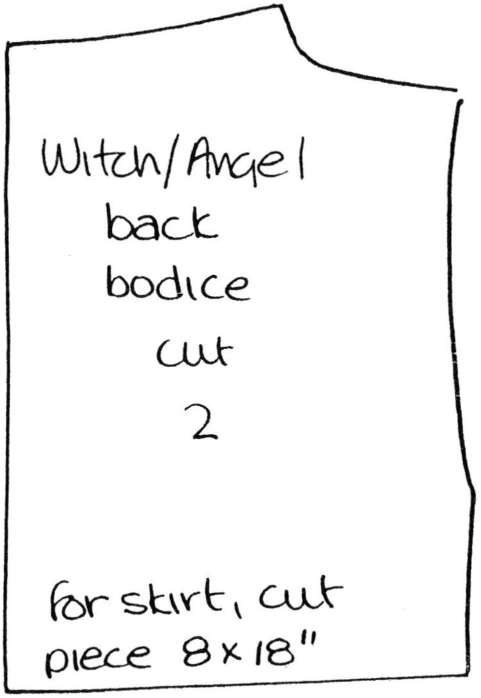

Witch/Angel
back
bodice
cut
2

for skirt, cut
piece 8 x 18"

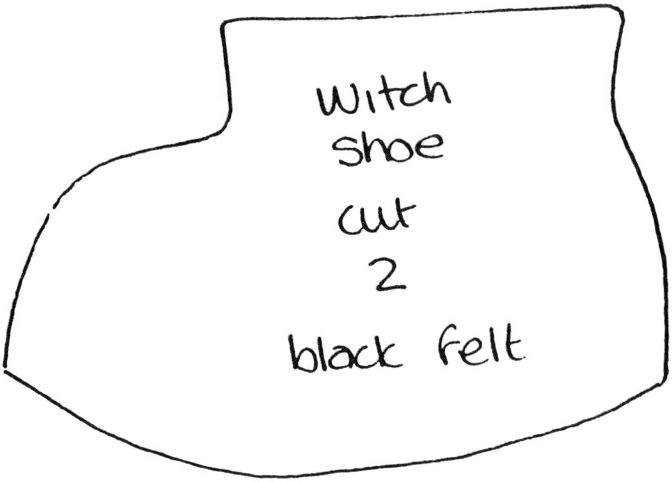

Witch
shoe
cut
2
black felt

Fig. 80. Shoe, back bodice, and buckle patterns for Witch.
More patterns for Witch can be found on pages 82 to 85.

Witch
sleeve
cut
2
black

Witch
front
bodice
cut
1
black

Fig. 81. Sleeve and
front bodice patterns
for Witch.

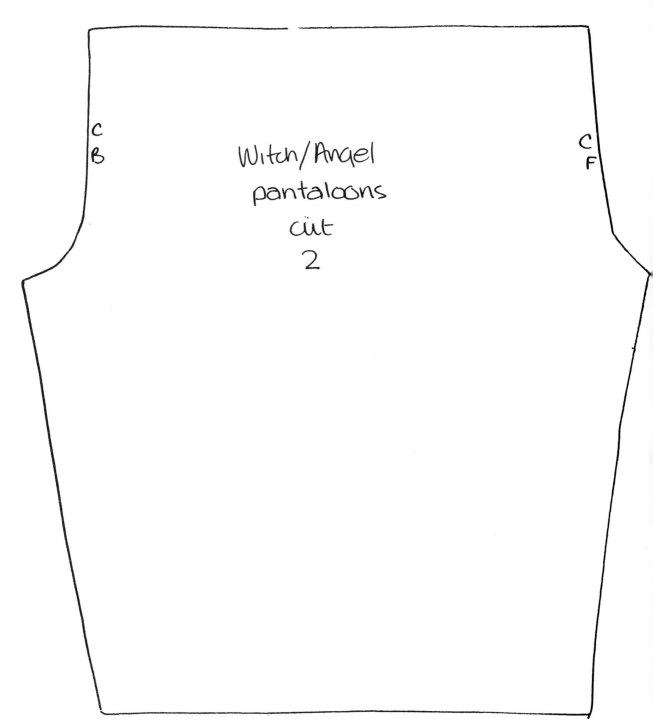

C
B

Witch/Angel
pantaloons
cut
2

C
F

Fig. 82.   *Pantaloons pattern for Witch.*

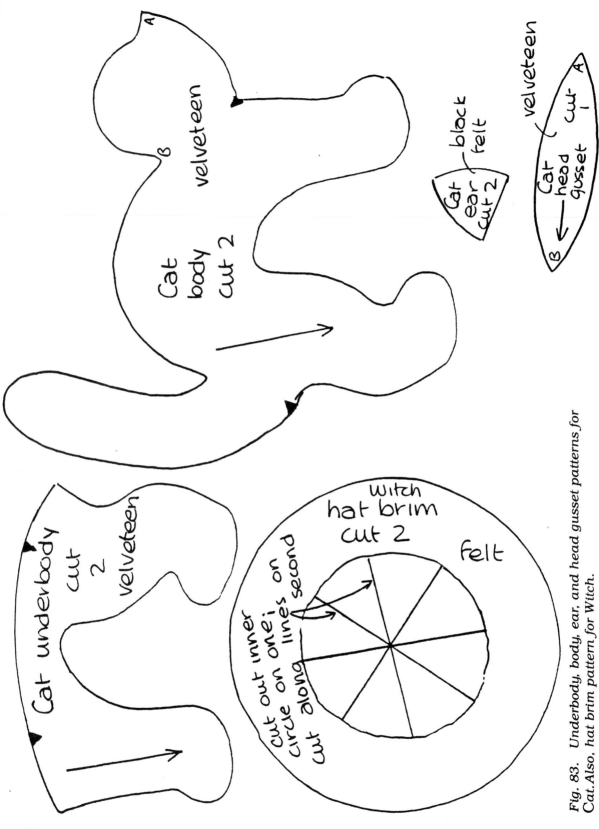

A

velveteen

B

Cat
body
cut 2

Cat
ear
cut 2

black
felt

velveteen

Cat
head
gusset

cut 1

A

B

Cat underbody
cut
2
velveteen

Witch
hat brim
cut 2

felt

Cut out inner
circle on one;
cut on lines
cut along
second

Fig. 83. Underbody, body, ear, and head gusset patterns for Cat. Also, hat brim pattern for Witch.

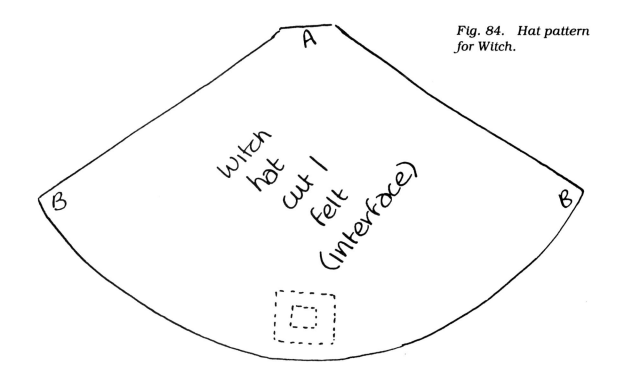

Fig. 84. Hat pattern for Witch.

Witch
hat
cut 1
felt
(interface)

ANGEL'S CLOTHES

PANTALOONS: Hem leg bottom with narrow rolled hem. One-half inch from bottom of leg, stitch gold rickrack in place. Fold leg so that only one edge of rickrack protrudes, giving scalloped trim with white below. Topstitch along edge of fold. Make pantaloons as for witch, omitting elastic on bottom leg edges.

DRESS: Stitch rickrack to edge of front bodice center. Fold edge under so that scalloped edge of rickrack shows. Topstitch center front bodice to front bodice sides along A-B. Make dress as described for Sonya, up to point of hemming skirt. Trim angel's skirt as described for pantaloons. Sew center back seam of skirt from hem to finished edge. Turn and put on doll. Sew snap fasteners to waist and neck edge.

WINGS: Trim curved edge all around with gold rickrack. Attach wings to back of dress so wings show sticking out from behind.

SHOES: Make as described for Sonya.

HALO: Make a loop from length of gold cord and sew together at back. Set on angel's head.

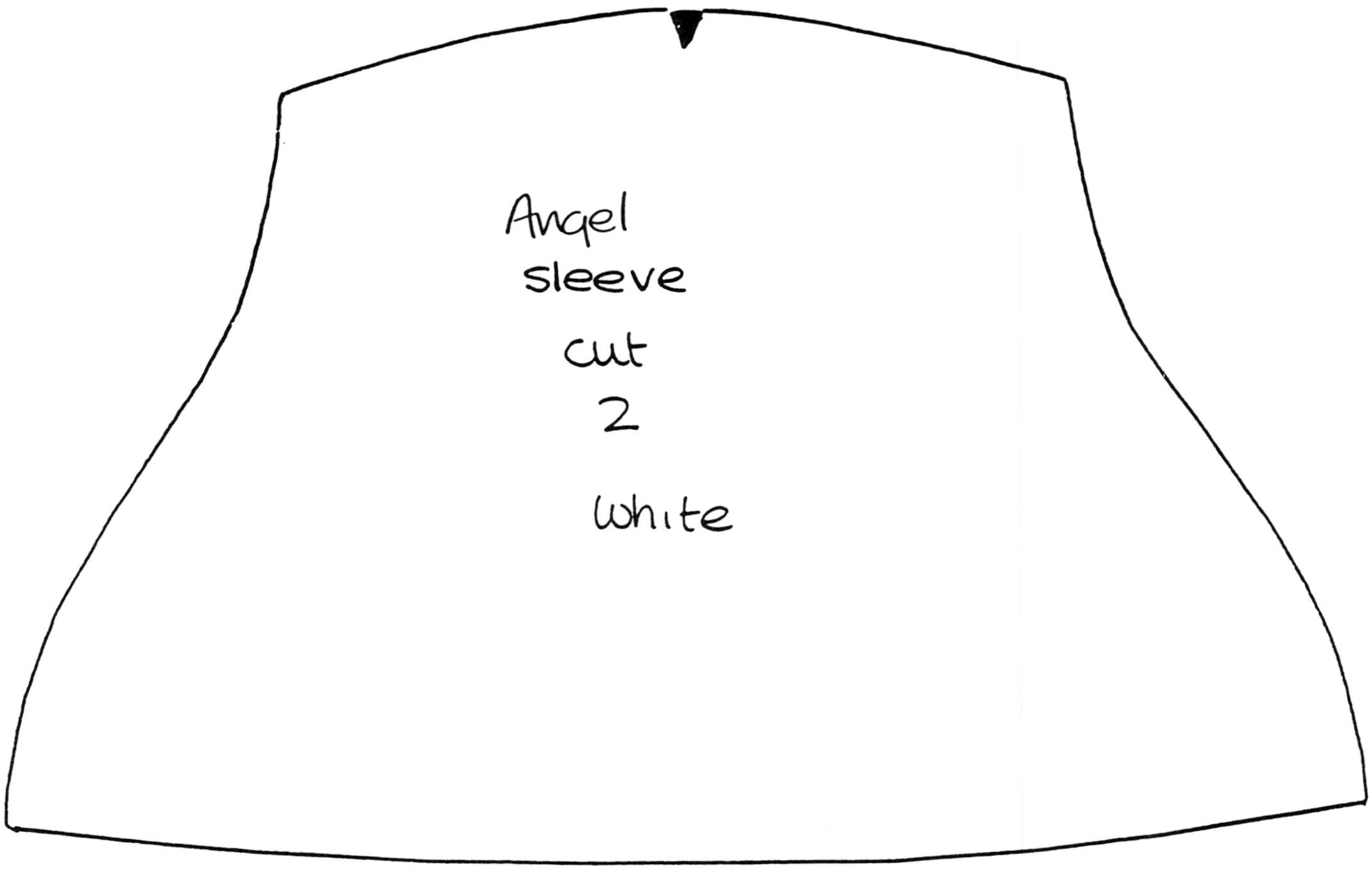

Angel
sleeve
cut
2
White

Fig. 85. Sleeve pattern for Angel.

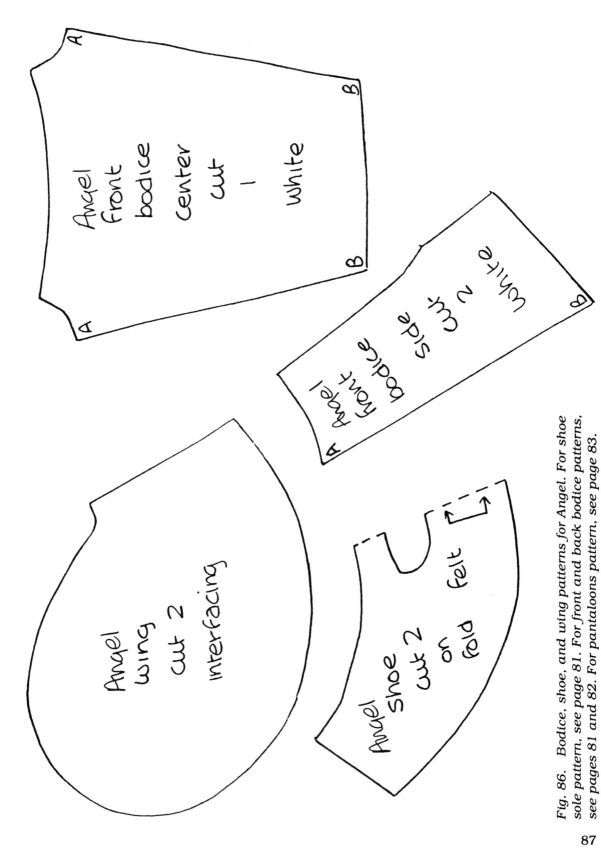

Fig. 86. Bodice, shoe, and wing patterns for Angel. For shoe sole pattern, see page 81. For front and back bodice patterns, see pages 81 and 82. For pantaloons pattern, see page 83.

The following labels appear within the patterns:

Angel Front bodice Center cut 1 white

Angel front bodice Side cut 2 white

Angel wing cut 2 interfacing

Angel Shoe cut 2 on fold felt

6 Beard Dolls

Unlike the dolls in the previous chapter, these ones are more decorative than functional. Some have bodies constructed entirely of felt, and most have realistic detailing.

These dolls show some of the variations which can be created from the genus of a single idea: in this case, characters with beards. Let's begin with the most popular bearded gentleman.

Santa Claus

Fig. 87. This jolly fellow and his constant sidekick— the Elf—are household favorites. Instructions for making the Elf can be found in Chapter 7 (page 116).

Material: *8 x 14" medium-pile fur, white, for hair*
16 x 21" red fur for suit
5 x 22" cream fur for trim
9 x 12" black felt for boots and belt
scrap of pink felt for face
5 x 5" green felt for mittens
scraps of gold felt for buckles
scrap of dark-pink felt for nose
1 medium jingle bell
7 oz. stuffing
1 pair paste-on moving eyes, 12 mm

HEAD: Stitch darts on top of hair piece. Right sides facing, stitch hair pieces together A-B-C-D-E-F, leaving open at bottom. Right sides facing, fit face into opening in front hair, matching points C-D. Stitch all around. Turn head right-side out. Stuff firmly. Brush hair out of way and gather bottom so that an opening approximately 1" in diameter remains. Set head aside.

BOOTS: Fold boots in half, right sides facing, and stitch front seam, leaving top and bottom open. Sew sole to bottom of foot all around. Turn boot right-side out and stuff firmly, moulding into foot shape as you work. Gather top closed. Set aside.

ARMS: Right sides facing, stitch trim to bottom of arm piece. Set aside. Right sides facing, stitch mitten from point G around thumb to point H. Open mitten out flat. Right sides facing, stitch mitten to bottom of trim on arm piece. Fold arm in half lengthwise and continue stitching from point H around hand and up arm seam. Clip corners. Turn arm right-side out and fill to within 1" of top. Set aside. Repeat for second arm.

BODY: Baste center front trim in place on front body. Topstitch in place close to edges of trim. Right sides facing, stitch body back to back legs, matching points K. Baste arms, facing front, in place on body front. Place body front and back together, right sides facing, and stitch down left side, leaving space open where marked on pattern, catching left arm in stitching. Pull arms through opening and stitch other side from neck to an-

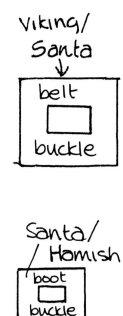

Fig. 88. Belt and boot buckle patterns for Santa Claus. Also, nose pattern. More patterns can be found on pages 90 to 97.

89

kle. Stitch inseam. Turn body through side opening. Stitch across body by machine just above crotch line. Stuff upper body firmly. Close side opening. Stuff legs firmly. Gather bottoms to close.

Ladder stitch boots to bottom of legs so that feet face forward. Glue buckle in place on each boot.

Fit head over neck and ladder stitch in place, face forward. Make nose by circle method and glue and stitch to front of face just above beard. Glue eyes in place on face.

SKIRT: Attach trim to side and lower edge of skirt as follows: Fold trim lengthwise, wrong sides facing, enclosing edge of skirt in between. Topstitch close to edge on right side, catching skirt edge so it's bound by trim. Attach skirt to body with hand stitching so it meets in front. Glue belt over join and top with buckle.

HAT: Bind lower curved edge as described for skirt. Fold hat in half lengthwise and stitch straight edge. Turn right-side out. Sew bell to hat. Stitch hat to head and fold over so it will hang to one side. Stitch to secure.

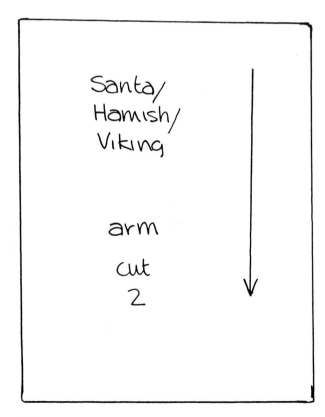

Fig. 89. Arm and hand patterns for Santa Claus.

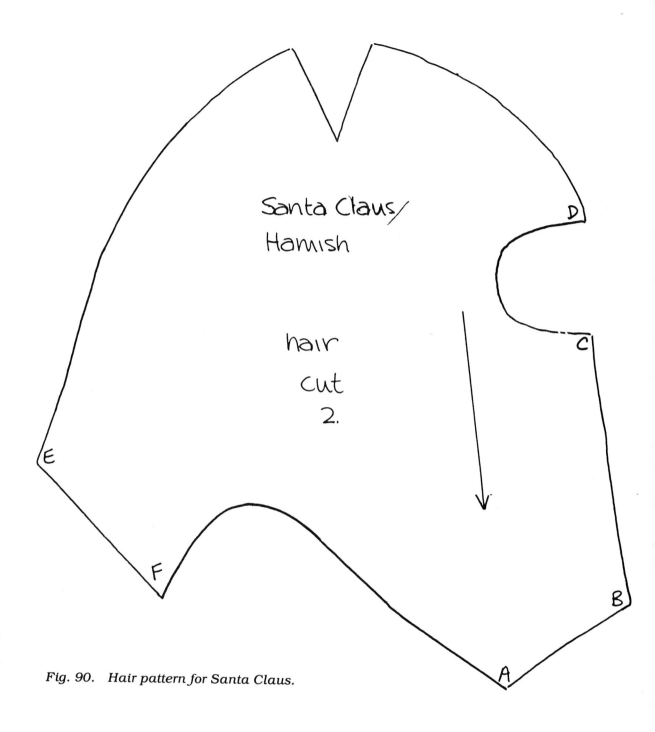

Santa Claus/
Hamish

hair
cut
2.

Fig. 90.   Hair pattern for Santa Claus.

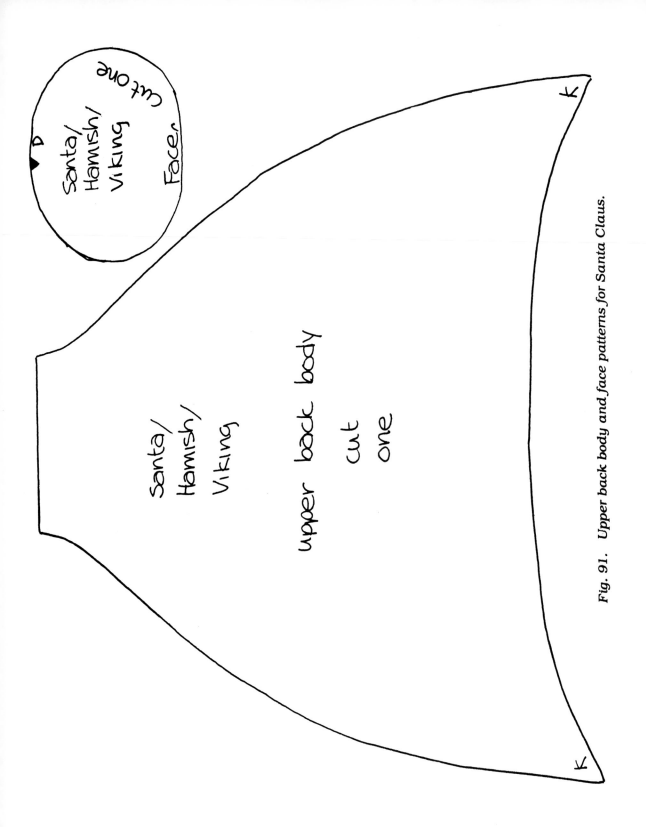

Fig. 91. Upper back body and face patterns for Santa Claus.

Santa/
Hamish/
Viking

Face.

Cut one

Santa/
Hamish/
Viking

upper back body

cut

one

k

k

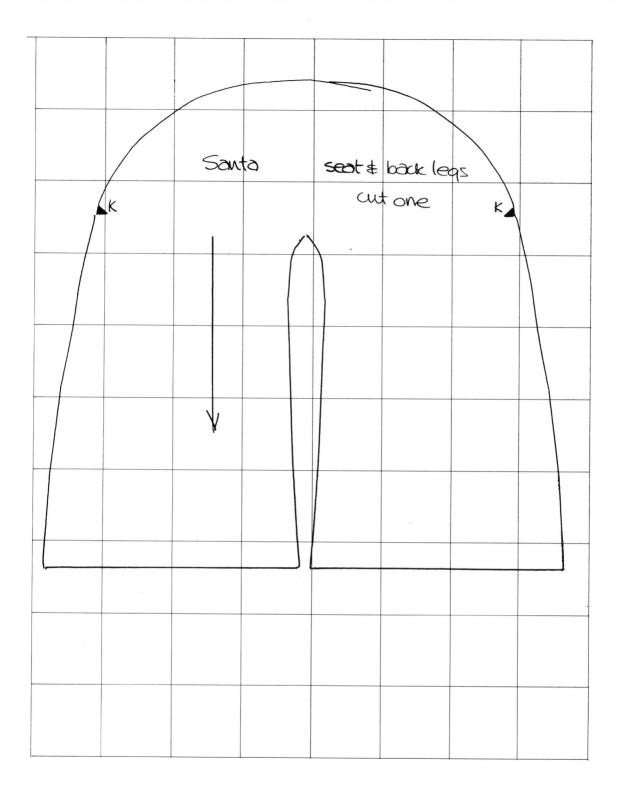

Fig. 92. Seat and back legs pattern for Santa Claus. Pattern is 75% of its original size.

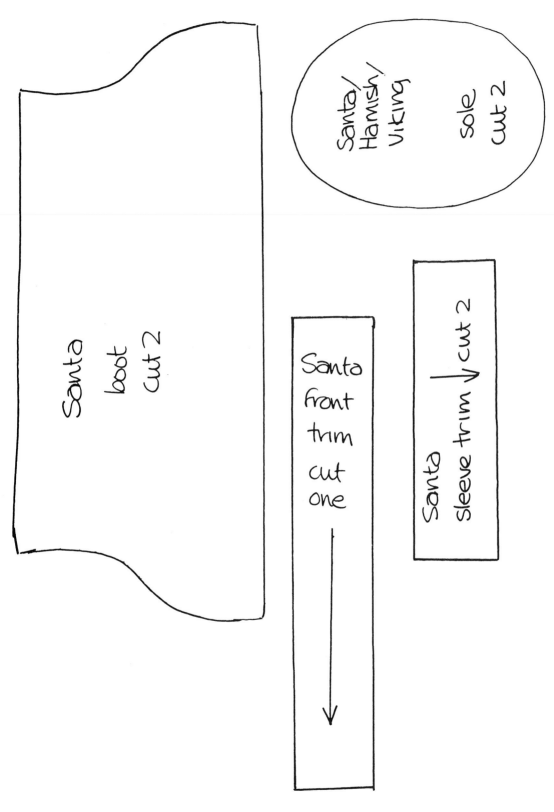

Santa

boot

Cut 2

Santa/
Hamish/
Viking

sole
cut 2

Santa
front
trim
cut
one

Santa
Sleeve trim ↓ cut 2

Fig. 93. Boot, front trim, sleeve trim, and sole patterns for Santa Claus.

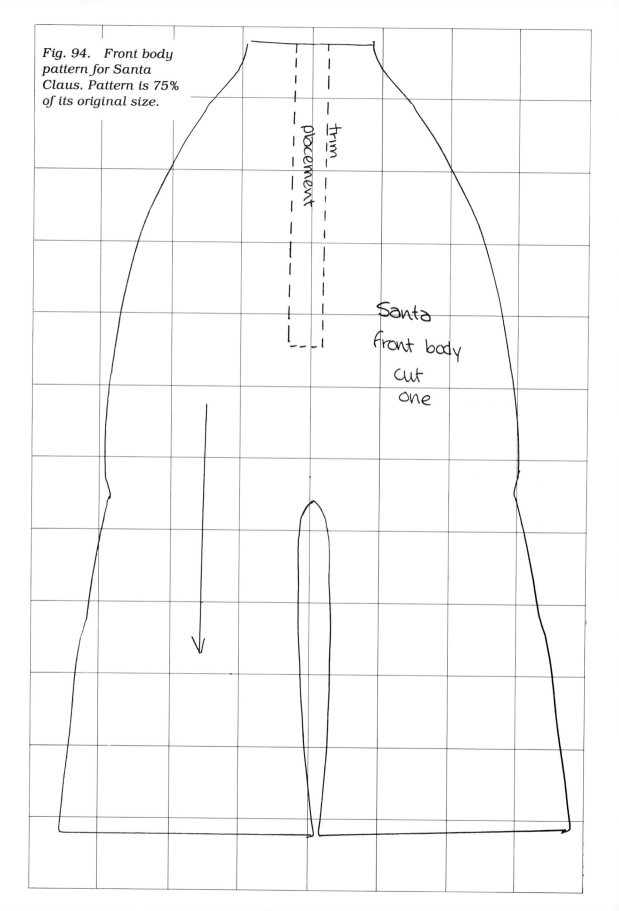

Fig. 94.   Front body pattern for Santa Claus. Pattern is 75% of its original size.

trim

placement

Santa
front body
cut
one

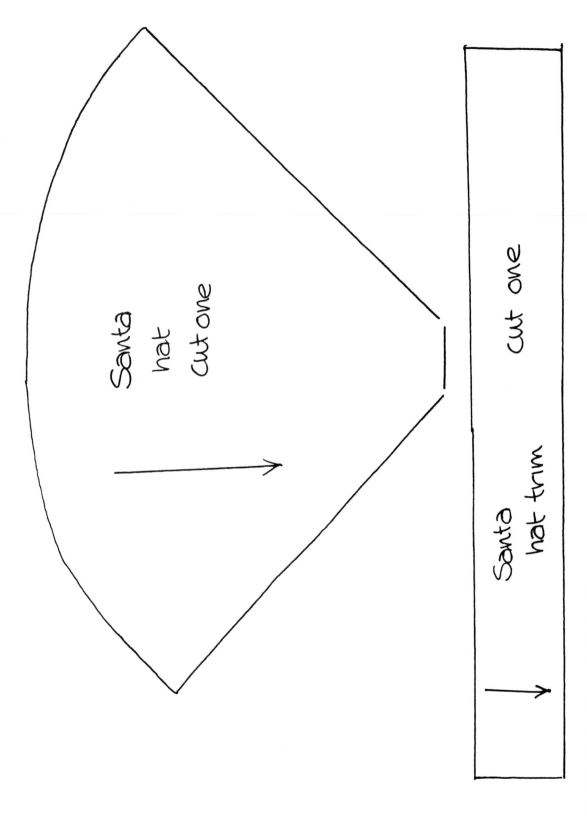

Santa
hat
Cut one

cut one

Santa
hat trim

Fig. 95. *Hat patterns for Santa Claus.*

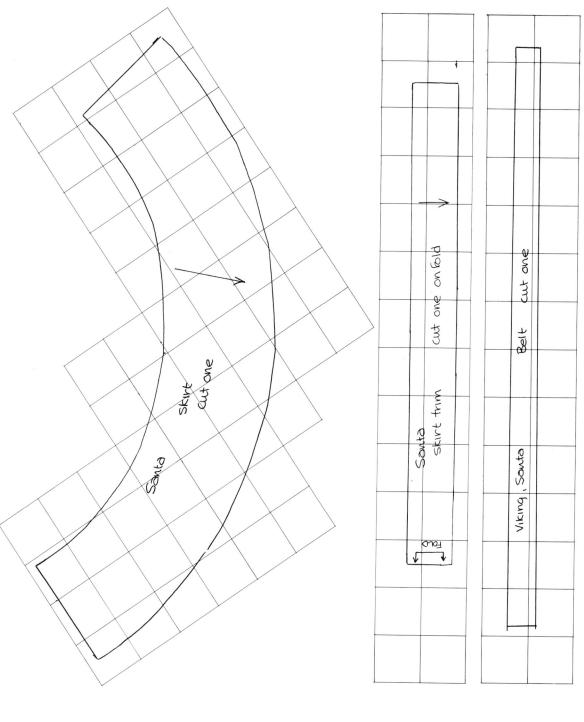

Fig. 96. Skirt, skirt trim, and belt patterns for Santa Claus. All patterns are 50% of their original sizes.

97

Hamish MacSporran

Fig. 97. Hamish MacSporran, a feisty Scot who does wear shorts beneath his kilt.

Material: 8 x 14" orange long-pile fur for hair
15 x 15" black felt for body top, arms, boots, sporran top
8 x 8" white felt for shorts
8 x 22" tartan for kilt, socks, tam
8 x 8" pink felt for face, hands, and knees
scrap of white fur for sporran
scrap of black fur for ermine tails
1 pompon for tam
scrap of dark-pink felt for nose

1 pair paste-on moving eyes, 12 mm
scrap of gold cord for sporran
1 small safety pin
6 oz. stuffing

HEAD: Make as for Santa Claus. Comb front of beard into moustache shape.

ARMS: Right sides facing, stitch hands together from point X to point Y. Open out flat. Right sides facing, stitch hand to bottom of arm. Fold arm lengthwise and continue stitching from point Y around fingers, and up back seam. Clip corners. Turn and stuff carefully, filling fingers first. Set aside. Repeat for second arm.

BOOTS: Right sides facing, stitch front curved seam of shoe. Open out flat. Right sides facing, stitch to sock. Fold lengthwise, right sides facing, and stitch back seam of boot. Sew sole to bottom of foot. Turn and stuff, folding top edge to inside. Do not gather. Set aside. Repeat for second boot.

BODY: Right sides facing, stitch body back to seat, matching points K. Stitch body front to front shorts. Baste arms in position on body front, facing front. Right sides facing, stitch knee pieces to bottoms of shorts on all pieces. Place body front and back together, right sides facing, and stitch down left side, leaving space where marked on pattern, and catching left arm in stitching. Pull both arms through opening and stitch down other side, catching remaining arm in stitching line. Stitch crotch seam. Turn and stitch across body just above crotch. Finish body as described for Santa.

Fit gathered knees into top of socks, with feet facing forward. Stitch carefully around top of sock. Glue buckle to front of shoe.

Attach head and finish face as for Santa. Comb front hair into moustache shape.

KILT: Top stitch all around 2 short and 1 long edge of kilt, ¼″ from edge. Fringe 3 edges. Kilt must be fitted to doll by pinning and pleating. Overlap kilt on front of doll, with left side over right. Form pleat on left of front so it forms a front panel. Pin pleat. Fold and pin back of kilt into small pleats until waist of kilt fits doll. Remove kilt from doll. Baste pleats in place and press. Topstitch pleats approximately 1½" down from top of kilt. Fold over top edge of kilt ¼" to wrong side and topstitch. Hand sew kilt to doll. Pin with small gold safety pin.

SPORRAN: Glue tails to front of sporran. Fold, right sides facing, and stitch straight edge A-B. Refold so point B meets seam line B and stitch curved edge C-B-C. Turn. Wrong sides facing, topstitch upper curved edge of sporran top, sandwiching cord in between so that ends protrude for hanging sporran. Fit furry pouch into top of sporran and topstitch across straight edge through all thicknesses. Attach sporran to front of doll.

HAT: Make by circle method, but do not stuff firmly. Flatten and stitch pompon to top. Sew to doll's head at an angle to one side.

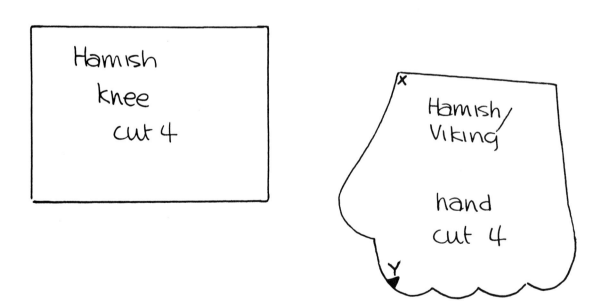

Fig. 98. Knee and hand patterns for Hamish MacSporran. For arm, hair, upper back body, nose, face, boot buckle and sole patterns, refer to the Santa Claus patterns on pages 89, 90, 91, 92, and 94.

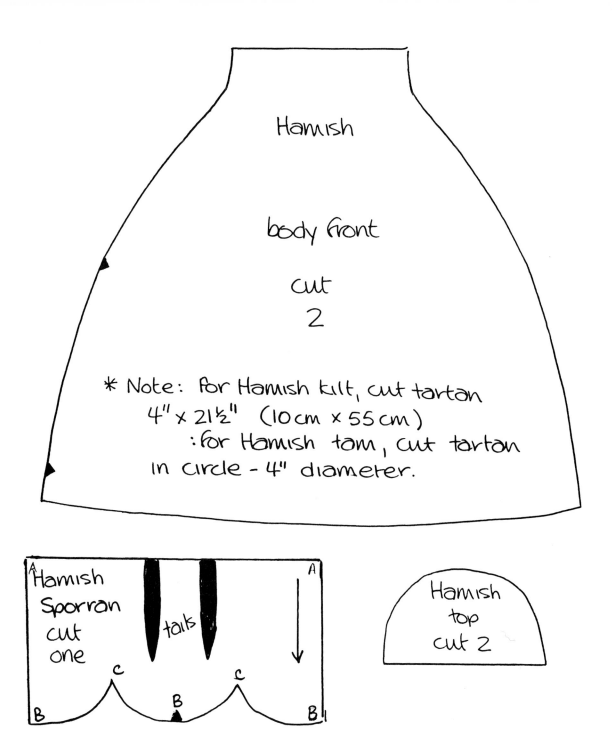

Hamish

body front

cut
2

* Note: For Hamish kilt, cut tartan
4" x 21½" (10cm x 55cm)
: for Hamish tam, cut tartan
in circle - 4" diameter.

Hamish
Sporran
cut
one

tails

A

B

C

B

C

B

Hamish
top
cut 2

Fig. 99.   Body front and sporran patterns for Hamish
MacSporran.

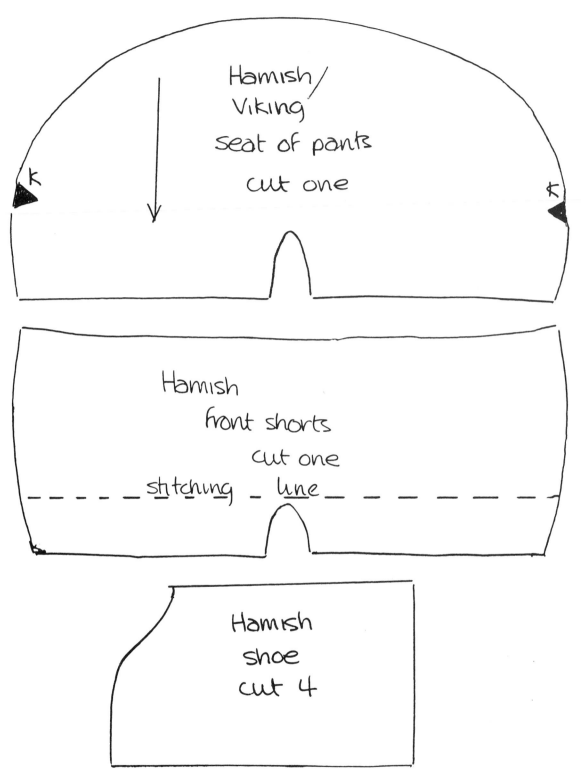

Fig. 100. Pants seat, front shorts, and shoe patterns for Hamish
MacSporran.

Fig. 101. *Stocking pattern for Hamish MacSporran.*

Viking

Fig. 102. This Viking—complete with helmet, belt, and boot lacings—is always ready for action.

Material: 8 x 14" blond long-pile fur for hair
20 x 20" tan fur for suit and boots
8 x 8" pink felt for face, hands, and knees
5 x 8" grey felt for helmet and buckle
3 x 13" tan felt for belt, soles, and bootstraps
scrap of dark-pink felt for nose
4 x 8" white felt for horn
1 pair paste-on moving eyes, 12 mm
8 oz. stuffing

Fig. 103. Horn pattern for Viking.

HEAD: Right sides facing, sew helmet piece to hair piece, matching J-M. Stitch darts in helmet. Finish head as for Santa Claus (page 89).

HORNS: Right sides facing, sew together in pairs, leaving straight edge open. Turn right-side out and stuff. Gather opening closed. Set aside.

ARMS: Make as for Hamish MacSporran (page 99).

BOOTS: Make as described for Santa (page 89), but do not gather top.

BODY: Right sides facing, sew back body to seat of pants, matching points K. Baste arms, facing front, in place on front body. Stitch side seams as described for Santa. Right sides facing, sew knee pieces to leg bottoms, matching notch C to side seam line. Sew crotch seam. Turn through side opening. Stitch across doll just above crotch line to form hinge for sitting. Stuff upper body and legs firmly. Close side opening by hand. Gather knees closed. Sew boots to knees as described for Hamish. Make boot lacings by gluing strip of felt around boot from back, crossing in front to back again.

SKIRT: Right sides facing, stitch side seams. Turn right-side out. Put on doll body and secure with hand stitches. Cover stitches with strip of felt for belt. Glue buckle to front of belt.

Attach head as described for Santa. Apply face in same fashion. Ladder stitch horns to side of helmet. Comb front of beard into moustache shape.

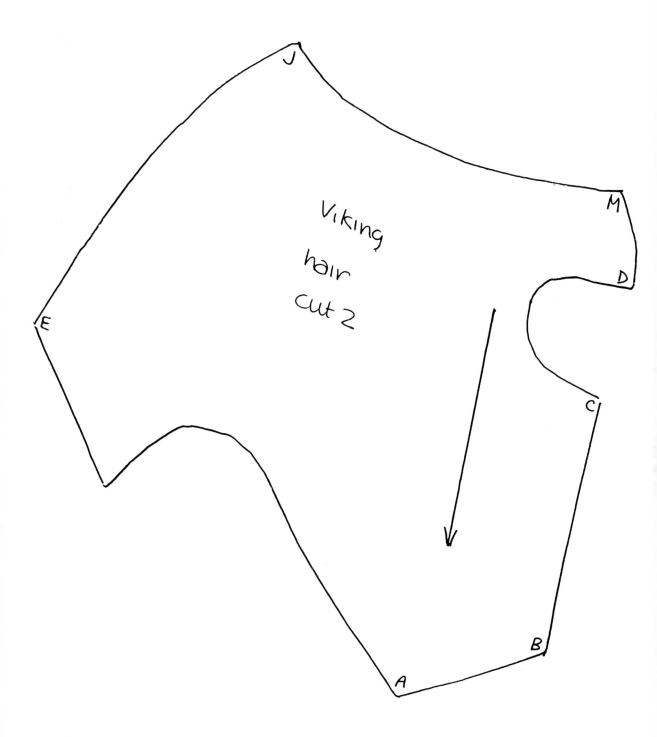

Fig. 104. Hair pattern for Viking. See pages 89, 90, 92, 94, and
97 for the following patterns: seat of pants; arm; hand; sole; belt
buckle; upper back body; nose; face; and belt. Additional body
and clothes patterns can be found on pages 106 to 108.

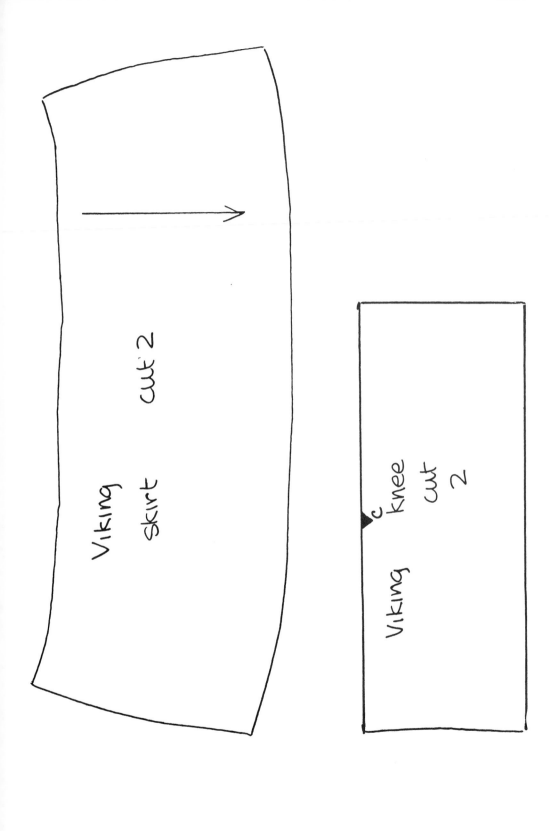

Fig. 105. Skirt and knee patterns for Viking.

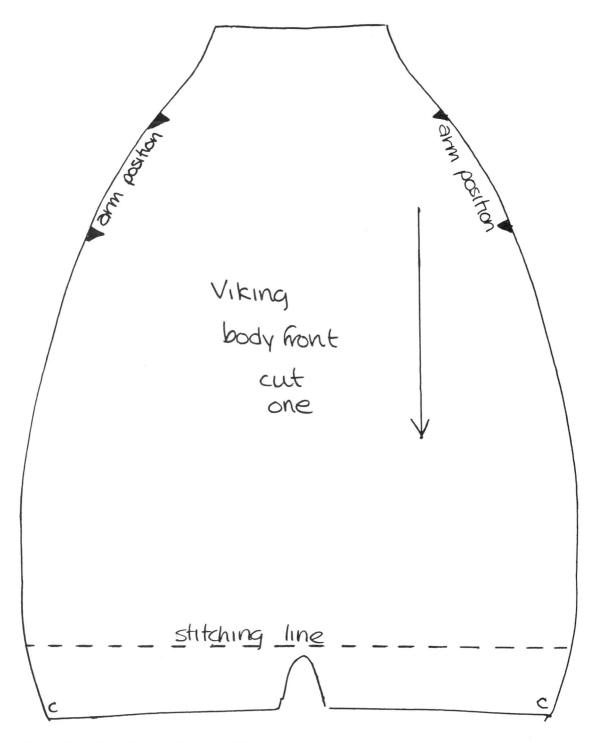

Fig. 106. Body front pattern for Viking.

arm position

arm position

Viking
body front
cut
one

stitching line

c

c

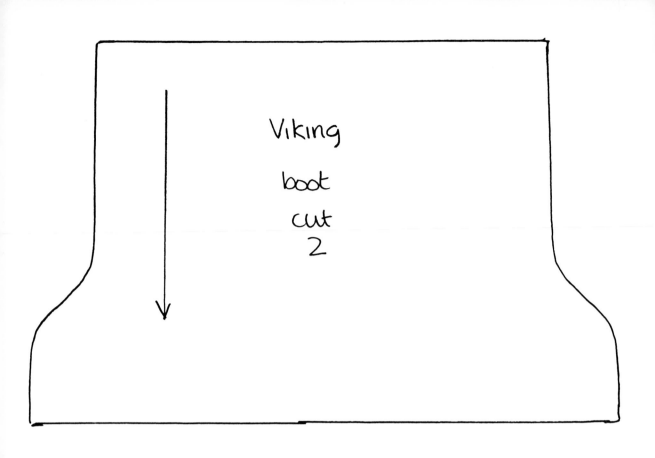

Viking

boot

cut

2

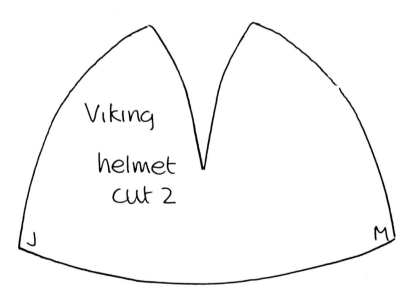

Viking

helmet
cut 2

J

M

Fig. 107.   Boot and helmet patterns for Viking.

7 Christmas Toys

No book of toys would be complete without a special section on Christmas. Some of the toys shown here are covered in previous chapters, but have been included here because they are thematically suitable. Christmas is a very special time of year for me, and I hope some of its magic has been imparted into the toys shown and described.

NOTE: Santa Claus may be found in Chapter 6 (page 88), Angel in Chapter 5 (page 75), and Snowman in Chapter 2 (page 20).

General Directions

For Christmas Decorations, trace around all pattern pieces onto felt with a marker or chalk, remembering to reverse those cut in pairs. Cut out carefully, just inside tracing line, so it won't show up on finished ornament. Stitch all seams with matching thread. All ornaments are designed to be hung with wire ornament hangers; if you wish to use braid, remember to provide long loops, instead of the short ones described, for hanging.

Christmas Decorations

Fig. 108. These lovely ornaments add a nice festive touch to the holiday season.

Material: Felt, small pieces (about 6 x 12") in red, white, green, brown, and white
scrap of white fur
scraps of felt in light and dark pink, black, and brown
trims: gold cord, gold rickrack, white baby rickrack
1 pair paste-on moving eyes, 10 mm
sequins of assorted sizes and colors
seed beads and jingle bell or pompon
small amount of stuffing

GINGERBREAD MAN: Place body pieces together, wrong sides facing, and topstitch all around about ⅛" from edge, leaving open between notches. Attach baby white rickrack all around by stitching in place on top of pre-

110

vious line of stitching. Stuff and insert small loop of braid into opening, and then stitch closed. Decorate with 5 mm sequins for eyes, nose, mouth, and buttons.

SNOWMAN: Place snowman shapes together, wrong sides facing, and topstitch all around close to edge, leaving open between notches. Stuff body. Topstitch through stuffed body on lines indicated to mark off arms and legs. Glue black hat pieces to head sides and topstitch all around, sandwiching head between, and leaving open between notches. Stuff lightly; insert small loop of braid into opening. Stitch closed. Glue mittens in place. Trim with 5 mm sequins for nose, eyes, mouth, buttons.

SANTA: Glue and appliqué cheeks in place on one beard piece. Place together, wrong sides facing; topstitch close to edge, leaving top open. Stuff lightly. Stitch hats together, right sides facing, leaving straight edge open. Turn. Place on head; stitch across through all thicknesses to hold in place. Glue fur trim to edge of hat on front. Topstitch all around. Make nose by circle method; attach to face. Glue eyes in place. Sew bell or pompon to hat end and fold hat downwards. Stitch to hold. Attach a metal or thread eye to top to accommodate ornament hanger.

STOCKING WITH BEAR: Place stocking pieces together, wrong sides facing, and topstitch all around close to edge, leaving top open. Cut length of gold rickrack to go around edge of sock, with small loop at top for hanging. Stitch in place over previous stitching. Trim front of sock with large and small sequins and spangles.

Make bear by gluing ears to wrong side of body piece so that curved edges protrude on right side. Place bear body, right-side up, on small block of felt. Stitch by hand or machine all around close to edge of bear, leaving open between notches on head, and catching ears in stitching. Trim away excess felt from back of bear. Slash between legs. Stuff bear lightly. Close opening. Make snout by circle method, but do not stuff. Attach to front of bear face. Embroider mouth with black thread and sew seed beads in place for eyes and nose. Glue small bow tie shape to neck, and slip bear into stocking.

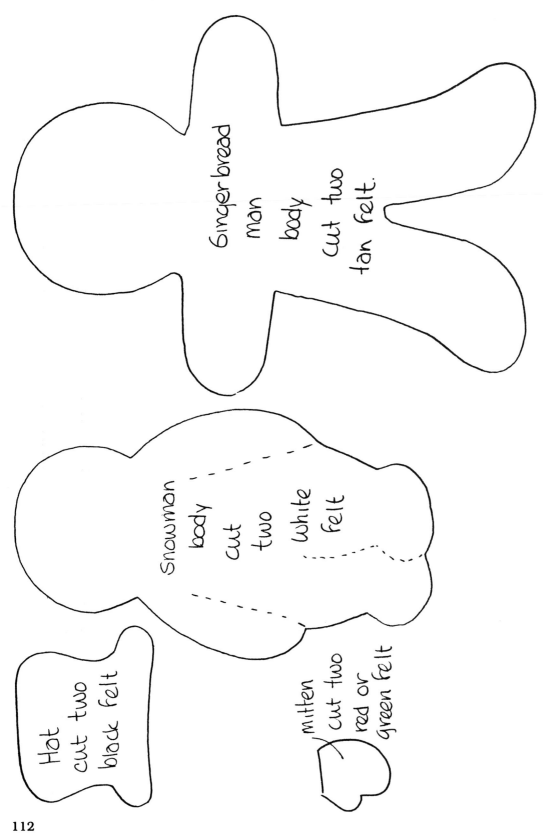

Ginger bread man body cut two tan felt.

Snowman body cut two white felt

Hat cut two black felt

Mitten cut two red or green felt

Fig. 109. Patterns for Snowman and Gingerbread Man.

112

Tiny Stocking cut two felt

bowtie cut one red felt

Bear body

cut two tan felt

ear cut two tan felt

slash after stitching

Hat trim ↓ cut one white fur

Nose cut one dk. pink felt

Santa hat cut two red felt

Santa face cut two white felt

Fig. 110.   Patterns for Stocking with Bear and Santa Claus.

Finger Puppets

Fig. 112. Beard
pattern for Santa
Finger Puppet.

Material: *5 x 5" each red and white fur for bodies*
scrap of white fur for beard
scraps of felt in black, green, blue, gold,
orange, red, and white
2 pompons, white and pink
1 plastic top hat

Hem bottom of body piece by machine. Right sides facing, stitch body back seam from A to hem, leaving bottom open. Turn. Glue features in place to make each character.

SANTA: Glue beard to front. Glue pompon nose in place. Make eyes of blue and black dots and glue in position. Glue strips of felt for trim and belt. Glue buckle in position. Glue green mittens to body front.

SNOWMAN: Make nose as described for small snowman in Chapter 2 (pages 7 and 8). Glue on dots for eyes, mouth, buttons. Glue red mittens to front. Glue top hat to head.

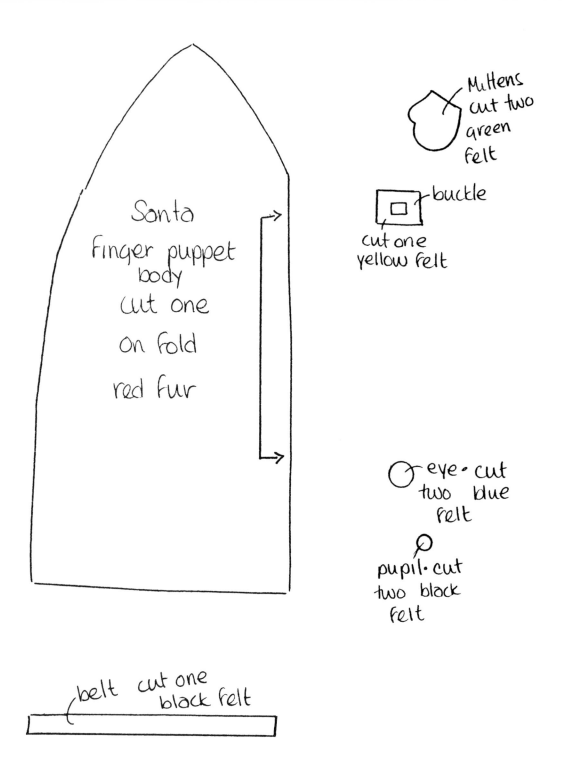

Santa
Finger puppet
body
cut one
on fold
red fur

Mittens
cut two
green
felt

buckle

cut one
yellow felt

eye· cut
two blue
felt

pupil· cut
two black
felt

belt   cut one
         black felt

Fig. 113.   Patterns for Santa Finger Puppet.

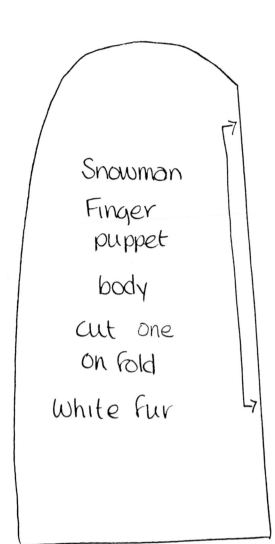

Snowman
Finger
puppet

body

cut one
on fold

White fur

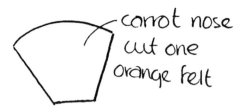

carrot nose
cut one
orange felt

Mitten
cut
two
red
felt

dots for
eyes, mouth
buttons
black felt

Fig. 114. *Patterns for Snowman Finger Puppet.*

Elf Doll

Material: *4 x 7" white medium-pile fur for hair*
5 x 5" pink felt for face/hands
9 x 12" red felt for jacket and skirt
9 x 12" green felt for leggings and hat
scrap of black felt for belt
scrap of gold felt for buckle
scrap of dark pink felt for nose
1 pair paste-on moving eyes, 7 mm
1 jingle bell and 2 oz. stuffing

EARS: Right sides facing, stitch together in pairs, leaving straight edge open. Turn right-side out. Insert raw edge of ear into slit in head side from right side of fur. Stitch slit closed, catching ear in stitching. Right sides facing, matching A-B, stitch hat to head. Right sides facing, stitch head pieces together from C-D-E-F-A-B-G-H. Insert face into opening in front, matching E-F. Turn head right-side out and stuff. Gather bottom so that a hole about 1″ in diameter remains. Set aside.

ARMS: Make as described for Hamish in Chapter 6 (page 99).

BODY: Right sides facing, stitch body back to seat, matching points C-D. Stitch body front to front tights, matching points A-B. Right sides facing, sew foot tops together along W-T. Right sides facing, sew top of foot to bottom of leg front, matching S-T-S. Right sides facing, sew body back to back legs, matching points K. Baste arms in place on body front, so that arms face forward. Proceed as for Santa, stitching side seams and crotch seam as described. Right sides facing, sew soles to bottom of feet, matching heels at point X. Clip between toes. Turn body right-side out through the opening. Stuff feet and legs firmly, taking special care to fill toes first. When legs are filled, stitch across body just at crotch line to form hinge so Elf Doll can sit. Stuff upper body and close side opening. Set aside.

SKIRT: Make as described for Viking in Chapter 6 (page 104).

FACE: Make smiling mouth just above beard. Apply nose by basic circle method. Glue eyes in place.

Fig. 115. Nose, hand, ear, face, and foot patterns for Elf. More patterns can be found on pages 118 to 120. See page 88 for a photograph.

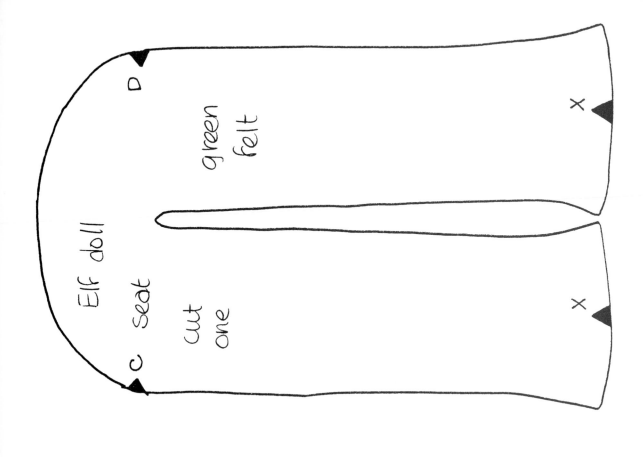

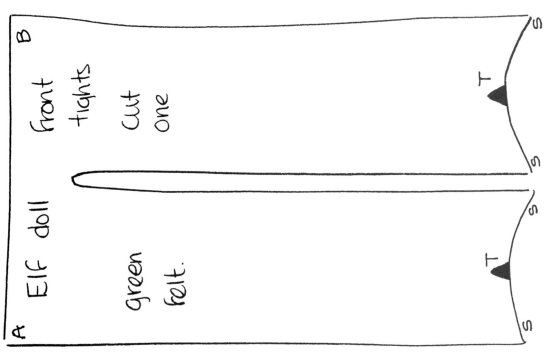

Fig. 116. Front tights and seat patterns for Elf Doll.

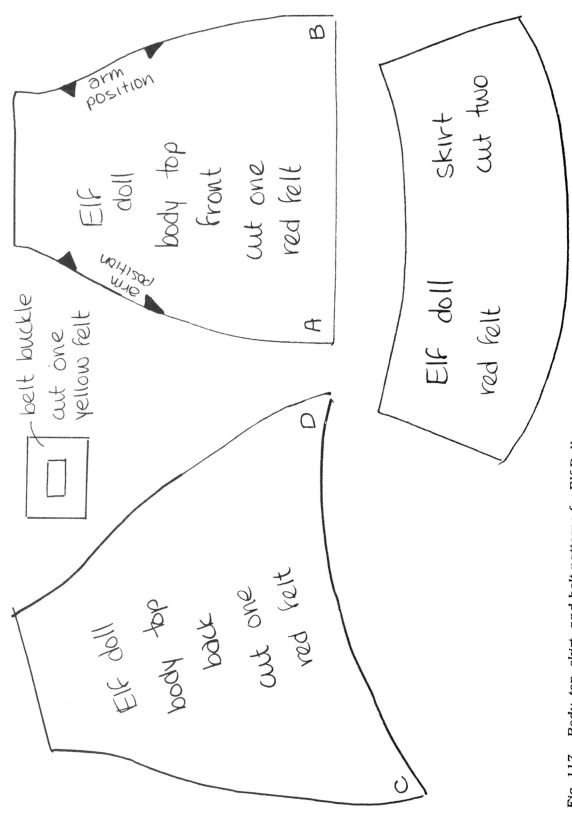

Fig. 117. Body top, skirt, and belt patterns for Elf Doll.

arm position

B

arm position

A

Elf doll body top front cut one red felt

belt buckle cut one yellow felt

D

C

Elf doll body top back cut one red felt

skirt cut two

Elf doll red felt

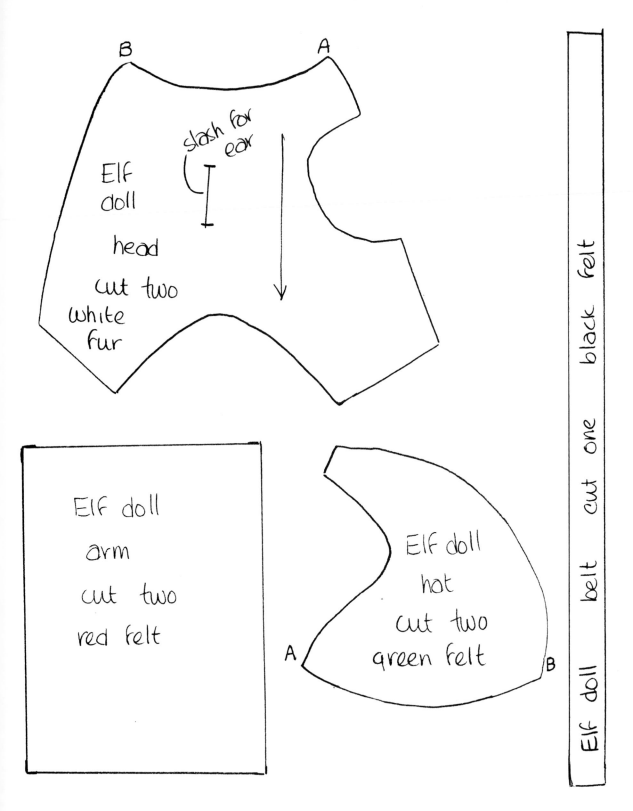

B

A

slash for ear

Elf doll

head

cut two white fur

Elf doll

arm

cut two red felt

Elf doll

hot

cut two green felt

A

B

Elf doll   belt   cut one   black felt

Fig. 118.   Head, arm, hat, and belt patterns for Elf Doll.

120

8 Lions and Tigers

Lions and tigers have such strong appeal to adults and children alike, they deserve a special chapter. These toys have definite human characteristics.

Lion

Fig. 119. Lions and Tigers are two very popular toys.

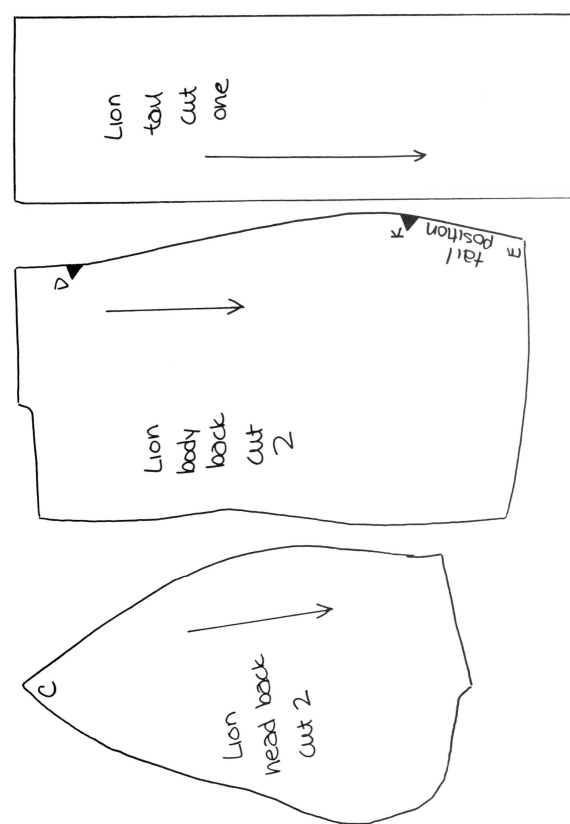

Lion
tail
cut
one

Lion
body
back
cut
2

tail
position

D

E

Lion
head back
cut 2

C

Fig. 120. Head back, body back, and tail patterns for Lion.

Material: *18 x 30" gold fur for body*

5 x 6" white fur for stomach, snout, and ear linings

6 x 8" long-pile brown fur for mane and cheeks

scraps of brown felt for nose bottom and paw pads

scrap of gold felt for nose top

scraps of white and black felt for eyes

8 oz. stuffing

EARS: Make as for Ernie Rabbit, Chapter 4 (page 45).

ARMS: Make as for Ernie Rabbit.

LEGS: Make as for Ernie Rabbit.

TAIL: Stitch tail tip to end of tail, right sides facing. Fold in half lengthwise and stitch from curved end along long edge. Turn but do not stuff. Set aside.

BODY: Make front as for Ernie Rabbit.

BACK: Right sides facing, baste and stitch head back to body back along neck seam, keeping mane fur out of stitching line. Stitch backs together along seam line C-D. Baste tail in place to one side of body back. Continue finishing body as described for Ernie Rabbit.

SNOUT: Make as for Ernie Rabbit, omitting teeth. Make chin as for snout.

NOSE: Sew nose top to nose bottom along curved edges. Turn. Stuff firmly; take large stitches across back, pulling sides in slightly, to hold stuffing in place. Apply glue (optional); sew in position, all around edges, to face.

EYES: Cut out large and small pieces in black felt, middles in white felt. Glue in layers together as shown on pattern, and take a stitch through all 3 with white thread to give highlights. Trim inner edges and glue to face.

Fig. 121. Nose and ear lining patterns for Lion.

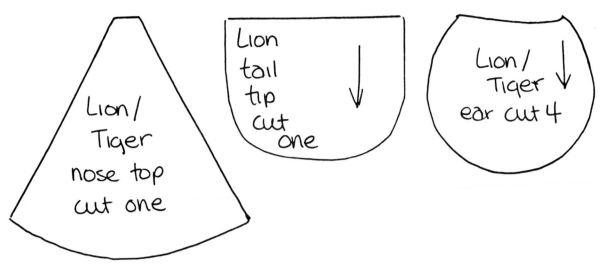

Fig. 122. Nose, tail tip, and ear patterns for Lion. See Ernie
Rabbit patterns (pages 46 to 50) for cheek, arm, sole, paw pad,
leg, body, stomach, head, nose, snout, and eye patterns.

Tiger

Material: 18 x 30" tiger-striped fur
6 x 8" white fur for stomach, soles, ear
    linings, and snout
small amount of brown felt for nose bottom
    and paw pads
scrap of light-brown felt for nose top
scraps of black and white felt for eyes
8 oz. stuffing

EARS, ARMS, LEGS: Make as described for Ernie Rabbit (pages 45 and 46).

TAIL: Fold in half lengthwise and stitch from curved end along long edge. Turn but do not stuff.

BODY: Make front as for Ernie Rabbit. Make back as for Ernie Rabbit also, but add tail. Baste tail in place to one side of body back, catching in stitching K-E. Continue finishing body as described for Ernie Rabbit.

FACE: Make as described for Lion.

Fig. 123. Tiger tail pattern. See pages 46 to 50 (Ernie Rabbit) and page 124 for additional patterns.

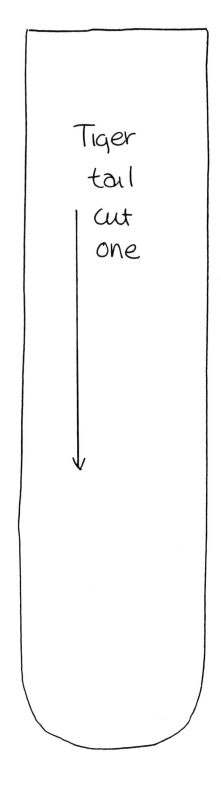

METRIC EQUIVALENCY CHART

MM—MILLIMETRES   CM—CENTIMETRES

INCHES TO MILLIMETRES AND CENTIMETRES

INCHES	MM	CM	INCHES	CM	INCHES	CM
⅛	3	0.3	9	22.9	30	76.2
¼	6	0.6	10	25.4	31	78.7
⅜	10	1.0	11	27.9	32	81.3
½	13	1.3	12	30.5	33	83.8
⅝	16	1.6	13	33.0	34	86.4
¾	19	1.9	14	35.6	35	88.9
⅞	22	2.2	15	38.1	36	91.4
1	25	2.5	16	40.6	37	94.0
1¼	32	3.2	17	43.2	38	96.5
1½	38	3.8	18	45.7	39	99.1
1¾	44	4.4	19	48.3	40	101.6
2	51	5.1	20	50.8	41	104.1
2½	64	6.4	21	53.3	42	106.7
3	76	7.6	22	55.9	43	109.2
3½	89	8.9	23	58.4	44	111.8
4	102	10.2	24	61.0	45	114.3
4½	114	11.4	25	63.5	46	116.8
5	127	12.7	26	66.0	47	119.4
6	152	15.2	27	68.6	48	121.9
7	178	17.8	28	71.1	49	124.5
8	203	20.3	29	73.7	50	127.0

YARDS TO METRES

YARDS	METRES	YARDS	METRES	YARDS	METRES	YARDS	METRES	YARDS	METRES
⅛	0.11	2⅛	1.94	4⅛	3.77	6⅛	5.60	8⅛	7.43
¼	0.23	2¼	2.06	4¼	3.89	6¼	5.72	8¼	7.54
⅜	0.34	2⅜	2.17	4⅜	4.00	6⅜	5.83	8⅜	7.66
½	0.46	2½	2.29	4½	4.11	6½	5.94	8½	7.77
⅝	0.57	2⅝	2.40	4⅝	4.23	6⅝	6.06	8⅝	7.89
¾	0.69	2¾	2.51	4¾	4.34	6¾	6.17	8¾	8.00
⅞	0.80	2⅞	2.63	4⅞	4.46	6⅞	6.29	8⅞	8.12
1	0.91	3	2.74	5	4.57	7	6.40	9	8.23
1⅛	1.03	3⅛	2.86	5⅛	4.69	7⅛	6.52	9⅛	8.34
1¼	1.14	3¼	2.97	5¼	4.80	7¼	6.63	9¼	8.46
1⅜	1.26	3⅜	3.09	5⅜	4.91	7⅜	6.74	9⅜	8.57
1½	1.37	3½	3.20	5½	5.03	7½	6.86	9½	8.69
1⅝	1.49	3⅝	3.31	5⅝	5.14	7⅝	6.97	9⅝	8.80
1¾	1.60	3¾	3.43	5¾	5.26	7¾	7.09	9¾	8.92
1⅞	1.71	3⅞	3.54	5⅞	5.37	7⅞	7.20	9⅞	9.03
2	1.83	4	3.66	6	5.49	8	7.32	10	9.14

Index

A

Angel, 75, 76–79, 80, 85–87

B

Backstitch, 10
Beard dolls
  Elf, 88, 116, 117–120
  Santa Claus, 88, 89–97
  Scotsman, 98–102, 103
  Viking, 103, 104–108
Bears
  in Stocking, 111, 113
  Tiny, 59–63
  with Vest, 51–58
Bee, 19, 20
Birds
  Bluebird, 30
  Chickens, 26, 27, 31–36
  Goony Bird, 22, 23

C

Cardboard, 6, 9
Chickens
  Mother and Baby, 31–36
  from simple shape, 26, 27
Christmas Toys. *See also*
  Angel, Santa Claus, and
  Snowman
  Decorations, 110–113
  Elf Doll, 88, 116, 117–120
  Finger Puppets, 114–115,
  116
Circle Techniques, 13, 14–15
Circle Toys, simple
  Bee, 19, 20
  Frog, 17
  Lady Bug, 18
  Mouse, 16, 17
  Snowman, 20, 21
  Spider, 18, 19
Closing up, techniques for,
  11
Cutting out, techniques for, 9

D

Dog, 37–38
Dolls
  Angel, 75, 76–79, 80, 85–
  87

Elf, 88, 116, 117–120
Fairy, 73, 74
Santa Claus, 88, 89–97
Scotsman, 98–102, 103
Teenagers, 64–72
Viking, 103, 104–108
Witch, 74, 75, 76, 77–84,
  85
Dowel, 6
Drawing compass, 7
Dressmaker's chalk, 5

E

Elf Doll, 88, 116, 117–120
Equipment, 5, 6
Eyes, 7, 8

F

Fabric adhesive, 6
Fabrics, 6, 7
Fairy, 73, 74
Felt, 6, 7
Finger Puppets, 114–115,
  116
Foam chips, 8
Frog, 17
Fur, fake, 6
  layouts for, 9

G

Gingerbread Man, 110, 111,
  112
Grain lines, 9
Grooming, 12

L

Ladder stitch, 11
Lady Bug, 18
Lady Bug Pillow, 24, 25
Layouts, 9
Lion, 121, 122–123, 124

M

Materials, 6, 7, 8
Metric Equivalency Chart,
  126
Mouse, 16, 17

N

Nap direction, 9
Needles, 5

P

Patterns
  enlarging and transferring,
  12
  tracing, 9
Pins, 6

R

Rabbits, 28–29, 30, 39–50
Running stitch, 10, 11

S

Santa Claus
  Decoration, 111, 113
  Doll, 88, 89–97
  Finger Puppet, 114–115
Scissors, 5
Scotsman, 98–102, 103
Sewing machine, 6
Shapes, simple
  Bluebird, 30
  Chickens, 26, 27, 31–36
  Goony Bird, 22, 23
  Lady Bug Pillow, 24, 25
  Rabbits, 28–29, 30
Snowman
  from circle, 20, 21
  Decoration, 111, 112
  Finger Puppet, 114, 116
Spider, 18, 19
Stitching techniques, 9
Stocking with Bear, 111, 113
Stuffing
  techniques, 11
  types of, 8

T

Techniques, 8, 9–12
Teenager Dolls, 64–72
Thread, 6
Thread snips, 5
Tiger, 124, 125
Turning techniques, 11

V

Viking, 103, 104–108

W

Witch, 74, 75, 76, 77–84, 85

About the Author

Jennifer MacLennan has been design-ing and making toys since childhood in Sydney, Nova Scotia. Since 1973 she has been designing toys professionally, and since 1979 has had several designs pub-lished in various Canadian publications. In addition, Jen has produced several original soft-toy designs in kit form and has taught soft-toy-making classes at home.